The Library Book Cart
Precision Drill Team Manual

The Library Book Cart Precision Drill Team Manual

LINDA D. MCCRACKEN
and LYNNE ZEIHER

McFarland & Company, Inc., Publishers
Jefferson, North Carolina, and London

Library of Congress Cataloguing-in-Publication Data

McCracken, Linda D., 1950–
 The library book cart precision drill team manual / Linda D.
McCracken and Lynne Zeiher.
  p. cm.
 Includes index.
 ISBN 0-7864-1159-7 (softcover binding : 60# alkaline paper) ∞
 1. Libraries—Public relations. 2. Libraries and community.
3. Marching drills. I. Zeiher, Lynne, 1952– II. Title.
Z716.3.M39 2002
021.2—dc21   2001044979

British Library cataloguing data are available

Front cover photograph: The Cart Wheelers from Lincoln Library wear the
green for St. Patrick's Day. *Back cover:* Cart Wheeler Annette Hunsaker.

Manufactured in the United States of America

McFarland & Company, Inc., Publishers
 Box 611, Jefferson, North Carolina 28640
 www.mcfarlandpub.com

To my husband, Coy,
for his support and understanding.

—Linda

To the Staff and Friends of the Peninsula Library,
the best in all the universe.

—Lynne

Acknowledgments

To the staff members of the Yakima Valley Regional Library Book Cart Drill Team, and to our library director, Anne Haley, who was proud enough of our group effort to send an article on our successes to several trade publications.

To Marvin Scilken, who read one of those articles and called for a longer piece for his *The U*N*A*B*A*S*H*E*D Librarian*. Unfortunately, Marvin died before he had the chance to see that article in print, and what it would bring about.

To Coy McCracken, for his loving encouragement and support.

To all of these people, and many more, thank you for making this book possible. Marvin Scilken always worked to ensure that "Libraries (and librarians) got the credit they deserve." I hope he would be proud of this book.

—*Linda D. McCracken*

I would like to thank all the great members of the Pierce County Library Drill Team who have volunteered their time, parade after parade and year after year. They have continually contributed their ideas, time and energy to create a fun experience that also works as a great public relations tool for the library.

Just as a book cart drill team requires the work of many people, this book has benefited from the efforts of many of the other library book cart drill teams from across the country. The libraries mentioned in the book have generously shared their ideas and experiences. They have sent stories, routines, pictures and sometimes video tapes. I would especially like to thank Kathy Falco from Ocean County Library System and Nancy Hunley from the Lincoln Library.

—*Lynne Zeiher*

Contents

Contents

· 1 ·

Our Parade Started Here: How We Got Rolling

Lynne Zeiher, Gig Harbor, Washington: Parades always seemed to have a special aura when I was growing up. I anticipated watching the grand parades on television. There was the Macy's Thanksgiving Day Parade with its giant balloons, the Pasadena Rose Bowl Parade with those gorgeous floral covered floats, and both had big shining marching bands.

They were fun to watch, but parade participation seemed a remote possibility. To actually be in the parade you either had to be personal friends with a gigantic helium filled cartoon character, Miss Hog Festival queen or at least a Pork Princess, or have enough musical coordination to be able to play music and walk at the same time. So I grew up always on the curb as the parade passed by. Sounds pitiful doesn't it? But some of us late bloomers never give up.

In 1996 the Pierce County Library (PCL) was preparing to celebrate its 50th anniversary. Since PCL is a branch library system covering a geographically large county, much of the celebrating was to be handled at the local branch level. By coincidence, the city of Gig Harbor, which my branch serves, was also preparing for its

50th anniversary that same year. There had to be some way to marry the two events.

One of the main elements of the city's celebration plans was a big community parade. If we could somehow participate in the parade, it could be a great way to combine our two celebrations, show the library's support for the city, publicize our birthday, and fulfill my dream of making it into a parade—a tripleheader.

So, at a planning meeting of the branch's Friends group, I suggested that we brainstorm some ways we could make a memorable appearance in the parade. One of the Friends, Randall Beth Platt, a successful writer and all around creative-type person, jokingly suggested that we could push our carts down the street. Eureka! Everyone laughed, the discussion moved on, but the somewhat warped wheels in my head started turning.

This idea had promise. It could work. No one would expect to see a group of librarians strutting down the street with book carts. Most people would be surprised that we ever escaped from our building, but just being there wouldn't be enough to be really fun and memorable. After all, lots of other groups would be just walking in the parade. We needed something more.

I remember those shiny marching bands and their high kicking drill teams. If they could look cool with tubas and pom poms, then we could make it work with book carts. We could spin them, dance with them, whatever we wanted, whatever it would take.

The next step was to convince others to be part of my crazy scheme. This was no easy feat. "You want me to do what?" was the response I heard most when I pounced on people with the idea. "Trust me. It will be fun," was my usual retort.

If there were a cart or two handy, I would improvise some simple moves to help them picture the type of maneuvers I had in mind. I would spin the cart and try to show how they could weave back and forth while moving forward.

I recruited a handful of people, about eight, from the staff and Friends to attend a practice. DiAnne and Mary, who always indulge me by laughing at my lamest jokes, threw aside their normally conservative demeanor and agreed to join the gang. Terry signed on and started getting in touch with her inner actress. Since then, she has taken to the stage with a local theater group. Of course, I couldn't let Randall Platt off the hook, since it was her idea in the first place.

The Friends president at the time, Judy, was a great sport about the whole thing, joining the group and providing us with a few bucks from the Friends treasury to cover our parade entry fee and minimal decorating expenses. Pages Jean and Pam, figuring they were book cart pros, took the rear position so they could critique everyone else's cart pushing techniques. Chris, another good writer and all-round creative type person, agreed to be my co-choreographer.

Chris and I met after work one day with a couple of carts and a wide clear aisle in the library. We tried all kinds of moves to see what would work. We marched up and down the aisle, turning the carts this way and that, going in different directions. We skipped, we twirled, we kicked, and we danced. We did wheelies (the wheels fell off some of the carts, so we discarded this idea).

We played until we had a few moves that worked and that we thought would look impressive. We gave the moves names and called the group together for a trial run.

In the beginning, the maneuvers were all based on working from one double line, so everyone found an empty cart and we lined up in the library.

Starting practices inside had several advantages for us. First of all, we live in the Northwest, where rain is prevalent. By rehearsing inside we didn't have to worry about inclement weather.

Second, we discovered that several moving carts are very loud, but a carpeted surface is much quieter than asphalt. In order for us to be able to communicate and work out our problems, the softened environment of the indoors was much preferred. Of course, we didn't have much room to maneuver, but it was enough to work out the kinks and see what worked.

Our number one rule was to have fun and not to worry about being too exact. Still, we wanted to give the impression of some order. We tried to count out maneuvers as we marched. We discovered early that carts don't move too fast, so we spaced out all our counts from 4s to 8s or often 16s.

Everyone threw in his or her suggestions on how to make each move work easier. We tried all the ideas, kept the ones that worked, and the others naturally fell away. Some moves we even tried in slow motion until we could get the timing and movements right, then we sped it up.

The hardest part was keeping from running over each other's heels and to keep from laughing hysterically as we crashed into one another when *left* was confused with *right* and vice versa. We had so much fun at the first rehearsal that it was easier to recruit more members for the remaining practices.

Soon we were ready to venture out into our parking lot for an after work rehearsal session. The few library patrons who came by in search of the bookdrop were very puzzled about our activities. Many of them asked what we were doing, but I don't think they understood even when we briefly described our plan for the parade. We received frequent curious looks and snickers. Some just parked for a while and watched. Everyone seemed very interested and amused, so it gave us courage to continue.

In the parking lot we first experienced the roar of cart wheels on pavement and added a whistle to at least start and stop each routine. The noise, or lack thereof when we stopped, inspired our trademark shushhhing move when we first practiced our pinwheel maneuver.

I also had to convince the library's administration that this would be a positive, worthwhile endeavor for our branch and the library. I needed to get an okay to use the library's carts, and also to perform this extremely unorthodox activity in the Library's name. Luckily, our director, Neel Parikh, is an adventurous, fun type who supports different ideas, especially if it involves bringing the library out into the community.

I promised that we would use the really worn carts and that they wouldn't be the worse for the wear, and hoped that this would be true. (They do seem to be holding up quite well.)

Since not everyone at the branch was willing to risk being seen with this somewhat goofy group, I tried to get these staff to support us with some of the behind-the-scenes activities. We needed people in charge of decorating the carts, constructing a simple costume and devising a means to transport our carts to and from the parade.

Bonnie, who is a great crafter and superior scrounger (kind of like those black market guys in all the World War II POW camp movies) hit the craft stores and Goodwill for supplies. She made some great metallic bows for the carts and scored a bunch of dollar tee shirts to match the color of the library's 50th anniversary shirts. That way, if someone didn't have the library's shirt, they would still look like part of the group.

Rosina provided a big van to transport the carts to and from the parade. In addition, she and her carpenter husband, Iver, devised some clever book props for our walk-along marchers to clap and twirl. (See Appendix B for instructions on how to make these.)

On parade day we were ready to go. Our carts were decked out with blue and white bows. We had simple color coordinated outfits, so we looked spiffy. Two kids (it's always good to have some kids on your team) were proudly carrying our banner out front to proclaim our identity.

Our extra cart with our boom box and musical accompaniment—a tape of Marion the Librarian from *The Music Man*—was manned by two of our favorite volunteers, Estelle and Barb. They even took it upon themselves to make applause signs, just in case we needed to encourage the crowd. And most importantly, we were a somewhat well rehearsed and decidedly enthusiastic group of marchers.

We reached the front of the staging area and hit the street rolling. The crowd greeted us with mixed but always positive responses. Many of the people recognized our faces and shouted out hellos. Sometimes they would even yell out, "We love the Library." Now how many times do you hear that on the street? Occasionally I would hear someone ask, "What is that?" which was usually followed by an unsure answer of, "I think it's the Library," followed by a few chuckles and applause.

But as soon as we started even our simplest maneuvers, the crowd would burst into laughter and cheers. They really appreciated that we had put some effort into becoming an entertaining marching unit. We were thrilled and flying high. When our routines occasionally ran amok, we just joined in with the laughter and had a great time.

One of the big lessons we learned in this first parade was the need for either a really loud—or a nonverbal—communication device. We had names for the routines, but no set order to perform them. Whenever there was a crowd, I would walk down the row, tell each person the routine name, and then run back to the front.

Combine this activity with walking backwards for a few miles (got to keep an eye on the team's progress), and you soon discover some muscles that you didn't know you had.

When we arrived before the judging stand, we stopped the show with our pinwheel routine, which included a move where we suddenly stop and shush the crowd. Everyone laughed and we marched on in triumph. By the end of the parade we were all pooped. Gig Harbor has some winding, hilly streets, so we had to really hoof it sometimes to keep up with the rest of the parade—but it was worth every step.

After storing our carts in the van, I returned to parade central to watch the awards ceremony. Our goals for the event had already been met, since I felt assured that we had made a memorable, fresh impression on our community. We had been fun and had fun. Still, I was hoping we would get at least a small prize for our efforts. The Chamber of Commerce, who sponsors the event, gives out plaques in all types of categories, including most humorous, best presentation of the parade theme, Mayor's Choice, etc.

One by one, the mayor awarded prize after prize. With each category I kept hoping that maybe we would have qualified for that prize, but it always went to some other deserving group. After the humor award went to another group, I thought the Mayor's Choice was our only hope, especially since I knew the mayor was a big library supporter. But, alas, a cute group of kindergarten kids got that award. (Told you it's a good idea to have kids in your group.) Oh well, we did have fun. And, after all, this had been the biggest parade in Gig Harbor history, with over 100 entries.

Then, to my huge surprise, the mayor announced that the Grand Prize for the Parade was awarded to the Pierce County Friends of the Peninsula Library Precision Book Cart Drill Team. Yahoo!

Throughout the summer, patrons commented on seeing or, amazingly, hearing about our wonderful parade entry. Our plaque hangs in a place of honor in the library. The following year we expanded the team to include members from the entire library system, and we have been marching in parades ever since—rain or shine. Boy, did we ever get drenched in one April parade. We've added new faces, new routines, and are always open to new ideas.

After our photo appeared in the October 1997 issue of *American Libraries*, we started getting requests from other libraries on how to do it. Since librarians are in the information dissemination business, we were very happy to share all our secrets with everyone who asked. Since then, library book cart drill teams have been popping up around the country, and I've even heard of one or two groups who did it before us. Chances are good, though, that most people in the country haven't had the opportunity to see a real, live library book cart drill team in operation. But if they do, they will probably remember it well and think about their library in a whole new, brighter light.

Since that first parade I've been in countless (okay, only seven) parades, but each one has been a great success for the library and a personal blast. It's so satisfying when you fulfill a life-long dream, especially when you can involve your friends in it too. Now, if only I could figure out a way to become a Pork Princess...

Linda D. McCracken, Yakima, Washington: In January of 1997 the Yakima Valley Regional Library hired a new director. For many years our library had been busy doing the usual library promotions: story times for toddlers, book talks to women's clubs, booklists and bookmarks. But Anne Haley, our new director, made it clear that one of our priorities must be new ways to promote our library. The trick was that there was no money budgeted for marketing projects; whatever we decided to do needed to be, well, let's be frank, CHEAP. Forget thrifty and go directly to cheap!

Then it happened. A picture of Lynne Zeiher and the Pierce County Library's book cart drill team appeared in the October 1997 issue of *American Libraries*. "That's it!" I thought. I picked up the magazine and walked into Anne's office.

"Look at this!" I said. "This looks like fun. I think we should try it."

Anne's response was right to the point. "Why not? Let's do it! What do you want me to do?"

It wasn't until later, when my excitement had subsided somewhat, that I realized that I had just "volunteered" to head this project. Just how that happened I'm still not sure. But Anne's enthusiasm and my ignorance spurred me on. I knew that I could find several people on our staff who would willingly join in such a crazy venture, and more that I could convince to help in other ways.

As Anne and I talked about the project, we knew that we wanted to include as many of our staff members as possible. That, and the lack of funds, would guide many of the decisions we were to make down the road.

I presented the idea at our next department managers meeting and, not surprisingly, was rewarded with enthusiasm and commitments to help.

My next move was to put in a call to Lynne. This was the best move I could have made. As you have read, Lynne and her cohorts had pretty much worked out most of the kinks already—and, luckily for us, she was most generous in sharing what they had learned. Not only did she share some valuable advice, but she shared the routines that they had worked out as well. No need to reinvent the wheel.

There were so many decisions to make: Who would participate? Which parades should we enter? When were we going to practice? And where? What should we wear? Who was going to do what?

One step at a time. We had no Friends group to draw on for help. But it really wasn't very hard to get staff members to participate. A few volunteered up front, no questions asked. Some needed a little persuasion. We invited all staff members to participate and received a very favorable response. Everyone was very pleased that the new Director and our Deputy Director were among the first to agree to our crazy undertaking. Not what some would expect from their library's administrative staff.

First question answered. We had eight people who were willing to forge ahead with this project. Several others volunteered to help with the project, but they didn't want to be in the drill team. That worked out well. We needed to have a banner to announce our fantastic parade entry. Enter one "crafty" staff member. She volunteered to head the banner project. We had some felt left over from another project that we could use. We ended up having "banner bees" in the staff room during lunch and breaks. Staff took a few minutes to sew a blue blanket stitch border. Our facilities manager made a pole to carry our banner—it even comes apart for easy transport and storage.

Now, which parades would we participate in? I knew that the local Shrine temple was very busy during the summer months participating in all of the local parades. I called their office and was given a list of all of the local parades, their dates and contact information. We looked at the list and decided on four parades for our first year. Our first would be in a small town in lower Yakima County. Only three months away. Not much time and lots to do.

Now, when could we practice? And where? Anne agreed that we could use a limited amount of staff time to practice. So we set our first practice for 8:00 a.m. one workday. We decided that the hallway in front of the library's auditorium was large enough for our first practice. We were going to walk through the routines without carts for now. Before our first practice, I tried to adapt some of the routines that Lynne had shared for fewer carts.

So, armed with photocopies, our merry band met at 8:00 a.m. What a great time we had! That first hour went so quickly and we had such a great time that we all knew this was going to be a great success. We laughed, we messed up, we forgot right from left, and we really enjoyed working together. That was the best part.

After that first practice we were jazzed. We were going to wow the crowds that would line the parade route in anticipation of beholding such a unique and talented group, and we wanted to look really sharp. We decided on white slacks (I know, not very flattering to some figures, but boy would it look great!), white shoes and any "library" or reading T-shirt. Almost every year there is a new T-shirt design developed for our local summer reading club. We all either had at least one of these shirts or could borrow one. The brighter colored the better. And to top it off, we rounded up all the "Reading Coach" baseball caps we could find. Another local summer reading club promotion. We would look sharp!

We took our second practice on the road, or rather in the alley. And did we ever draw a crowd. One of the local police officers stopped to see what was going on. The bystanders might not have been impressed with our somewhat-improved routines, but they seemed to be fascinated by the very concept—can you imagine LIBRARIANS doing such a crazy thing!

One more practice before our first parade, and we were ready. We had chosen one of the smaller towns in the Yakima Valley to debut our fabulous drill team. It's a very friendly town, full of library supporters, and glad to have unusual entries in their local parade.

Parade day dawned dreary and damp, but nothing was going to get us down. We loaded our book carts in the library's delivery van, made sure everyone had a ride, and headed out.

The parade was a blast! The crowd started applauding even before we began our routines. Everyone enjoyed our drill team, even if we weren't perfectly synchronized! And the more the crowd applauded, the more energetic we got. That first parade is almost a blur; it was over before we knew it. And we were already looking forward to our next "gig."

A bigger town, and a bigger parade. We all had butterflies as we lined up for the parade. The local librarian had agreed to help carry the banner. Someone the local people knew and loved—couldn't hurt! Again we had a great time. One of our staff members video-taped our appearance, the parade announcer was very enthusiastic about our entry, and the drill team members again had a good time working together.

That was on Saturday. The mail arrived on Monday morning, and there was a package waiting. I assumed it was another unsolicited book from a publisher. Imagine my surprise when I opened the package to find an award from the parade. We had won a first-place trophy in the adult marching category. Truthfully, I think we were the *only* adult marching unit in the parade. But we took it as a sign that we were destined for even greater things. They haven't materialized, but we remain ever hopeful.

Our last parade of the season was in Yakima. We had hit the big time. The crowd was very supportive with their applause and hurrahs. But the parade took its toll on us. It was a very long, very mechanized parade. Almost everyone was riding in or on something. We had to really work to keep up, and about three-fourths of the way through the parade, one of our merry band had to quit from exhaustion.

As we talked together after the parade, we shared our frustration and disappointments. But we also worked through some of the problems that we had and knew that we would do it all over again, with just as much enthusiasm and fun as we had had before.

· 2 ·

Why a Book Cart Drill Team? Good Reasons for Stepping Out

Public Relations

Think about the most challenging issues facing public libraries today. No, not the Internet or shrinking budgets. Even before these issues began dominating the minds of librarians and administrations, we have been searching for ways to attract more people to the library. Once people come in the door, we have accomplished the hardest half of our task. Finding the key to reaching those who have yet to discover the treasures of the library has been a challenge for most of us.

Some non-library users may be intimidated by the old image of libraries as ivory towers with undecipherable codes and strict old ladies with tight buns in their hair who demand absolute silence. They may be intimidated by the new technologies they now find in their local library. Or maybe they don't even think about the library at all.

How can librarians change outdated impressions and replace them with a memorable, positive and even inviting image? Images that will be so different that they will shake up these stereotypes and banish them forever, plus do it somewhere outside of the library building where we can show off our best stuff.

The answer may well be a library book cart drill team. They can go where few librarians have gone before and do what few librarians—or anyone else—have done before. Library book cart drill teams take a normal and somewhat unnoticed tool, the book cart, and transform it into a rolling, stereotype-busting billboard.

The members of the team dispel that old stodgy image and appear as friendly, fun-loving people. They look like real people that a guy or gal could go to for assistance. Those non-users will be amused and, maybe for the first time, interested in just what might be going on in that well-kept building downtown or in their neighborhood. The next time they read an article in the local paper about a library event or library services, they may remember the drill team and decide to "check it out."

The drill team may be able to reach those audiences that you want to invite into your library. When participating in parades, the library book cart drill team is seen by families with children of all ages. Community leaders are also frequent parade participants and planners. Ethnic festivals bring out what can be a difficult population to reach.

The library's current customers will be excited and proud when they see their friendly local librarians in their community's big parade. Be prepared for lots of waves and cheers. Their enthusiasm will spread to others in the crowd and pump up the book cart drill team members as well.

Stereotype Busting

We librarians are all aware of what the stereotypical librarian is like. She certainly would never be seen pushing that rumbling book cart anywhere but through rows and rows of library shelves. A book cart drill team? How unseemly for someone of his/her station to be seen behaving in such a manner—and in public, no less!

That's part of the thrill of a drill team. For once, we librarians have the opportunity to get out of those library stacks, put on our sneakers and casual clothes, and strut our stuff for a surprised and very appreciative audience. People might get the idea that we librarians are just like them: We can laugh at ourselves and have a great time participating in community events. But be prepared—once they begin to see us as regular people, they may start coming into our libraries. And who knows where that will lead!

Building Teamwork

When you begin your book cart drill team, you may be the lone voice in the wilderness. In many libraries we may even feel that way about our jobs. By your team's first performance, however, you will have involved many more people. Just getting the drill team started will require lots of help. And just as the name says, it really is a "team."

Working on any special project will bring individuals together for a common purpose. What better way to promote teamwork within your library than a project that will be fun for the participants and for the community as a whole? That sense of team spirit will transfer into the workplace. Connections that people have made through the drill team can encourage cooperation on the job. You may find that people are talking together for the very first time—even though they've worked side by side for several years.

Building Morale

Take a group of people working together. Add an activity new to everyone. Stir in a generous helping of laughter. Mix well. Blend every few days until the big event. No matter what happens on parade day, keep smiling and enjoying the pleasure your book cart drill team brings the crowd. This is the recipe for a real morale booster.

The more people from your library that you can convince to participate in your drill team, the wider the ripples of laughter and fun will spread throughout your organization. This new activity is unusual enough that team members will have to step out of their normal work roles and relate to each other in new—and definitely fun—ways.

These changes can bring about a real boost in the morale at your library. Colleagues who may not have known each other before will share new and fun experiences. The library's friends and customers involved in the drill team will have a new way to relate to library staff. And the community as a whole will see their librarians in a whole new light.

Competitive Spirit

The newfound pride in your precision drill team will almost naturally translate into a competitive spirit. Who in their right mind would not judge this unique, fun, enthusiastic drill team as the very best ever to grace the streets of your community! What parade official could possibly deny that your library's precision book cart drill team deserves the highest prize given by the parade!

We librarians too often hide our talents or feel unappreciated. When the applause and cheers start, we certainly enjoy the attention and welcome the chance to show off our new skills.

That competitive spirit will build with each event your team participates in, and will gradually attract the attention of those staff members who were reluctant to get involved. You may find that you have more and more willing volunteers.

For Your Own Reasons

What are your reasons for starting a book cart drill team? What is it that you want to accomplish? We have presented some idea of what may happen once you bring some energetic, creative people together and turn them loose with those pesky, rattling book carts. Keep in mind that there are as many variations as there are drill teams. Each one has its individual goals. Those presented here are merely possibilities.

Develop your own goals. Write them into your plan. Share those goals with your administration and with the team members. Begin your new adventure together.

· 3 ·

Taking It to the Streets and Elsewhere: Opportunities to Perform

All the world's a stage—or a parade ground if there is enough room to maneuver. Of course, every area is different, but there are numerous performance venues where you can showcase your new book cart drill team. Sic the reference librarians on finding the best locations. It can be their contribution to the team effort.

Parades

The most obvious may be the community parade. Cities and towns of all sizes celebrate with local parades. Often the parade is the center attraction of some larger festival or holiday, and therefore may have a theme that can serve as the inspiration for decorations, costumes or even a name for your team.

Bright Lights, Big City

There are advantages to both the large and small parades. Larger parades with enormous floats and big bands will also have a large audience, even when the weather doesn't cooperate. Television coverage is a strong possibility. (When was the last time your library was on the small screen?)

On the downside, a parade that is heavily motorized may have a speedy pace. Without a motorized book cart, keeping up may require a drill team to really hoof it.

Chances are exceedingly good that the book cart drill team will be a unique entry in any parade and therefore an attention-getter. However, in a big parade it will be more difficult to get the attention that the drill team deserves. Larger parades may also be more selective in the type and size of entries. Although it is doubtful a parade would turn down the local library, be sure the drill team can make the cut before spending hours preparing.

Small-Town Hospitality

Small-town parades have their own special charm. The audience may be smaller, but if the group has staff members from that town's library, it is almost assured that the library's supporters will be lining the streets. Friends and neighbors will really cheer you on all along the parade route. They also can serve as a great training ground for testing out new maneuvers before moving up to the big city.

Another advantage to the smaller parades can be fewer restrictions and requirements. Big motorized parades often limit stationary maneuvers to one area, usually in front of the grandstand (and the television cameras). They may also require special insurance for motorized vehicles. Groups that contain children may also need to sign disclaimers or gain parental signatures.

Library Staff Functions

Performing at a library function can accomplish several goals. First, it's a great place to debut a recently formed book cart drill team. Having an audience of friendly, familiar faces can help reduce the butterflies that can accompany a first performance.

It can also help staff who aren't participating in the team to understand what is happening. Remember how hard it was to describe what a library book cart drill team is. If a picture is worth a thousand words, a moving demonstration should be worth at least a million. By showing everyone how fun and easy it is, other staff may become inspired to join, making the performance double as a recruiting tool.

Staff Meetings

Look for opportunities when all or a significant number of staff members are present. Staff meetings often need a short diversion or break from the usual activities. They also have the advantage that all the members of the team will already be present; plus, if it is held in the library or processing center, carts will be handy.

Picnics and Parties

Staff parties and picnics also present possibilities with potential for performances. Organizers of a staff Christmas party or other functions may be looking for entertainment ideas. The library book cart drill team can be the headliner. Decorate the carts with the appropriate theme and be the life of the party.

One of the obstacles to meeting and party performances can be the lack of appropriate space. The picnic grounds may have large fields, but the carts won't roll well on grass. Consider using a parking lot, tennis court or basketball court if the weather permits an outdoor presentation.

Finding a large enough space indoors is often more difficult, so be sure to check out the available space and practice in a similarly sized area. An indoor scenario will also require a revision in a parade team's routines to accommodate the non-linear arrangement of the room. This can easily be accomplished by combining a few stationary routines and removing the forward moving ones.

3. Taking It to the Streets and Elsewhere:

A Great Salute to a Retiree

If you are looking for a unique send-off for a staff member, especially a page or book cart drill team member, consider a cart tribute. There are a number of routines that adapt well to an indoor performance at a party. The biggest requirement is having enough clear space in which to perform the maneuvers.

When the development officer of the Pierce County Library took an early retirement to RV around the country, she was the first to receive our six-cart salute. Since she had been instrumental in enlarging our initial drill team to system size, she truly rated a book cart drill team send-off. To immortalize her, a special team of six carters assembled for her retirement dinner, which was held in our large meeting room (a big space was reserved for our performance).

To ensure her complete and thorough enjoyment of our special show, Sallie was perched on the top of a stepladder. (Parade formations like the ones planned are best viewed from on high. The ladder's presence kept everyone, especially Sallie, guessing throughout dinner.)

We entered the room chanting softly, "Sallie, Sallie, Sallie..." We immediately formed our six carts into the letter "S" and shouted out "S" as soon as it was completed. The bottom part of the "S" then lead the group around, which angled into an "A" formation. Everyone shouted "A." (Get the idea?) Next came the "L." Then, by the team moving three steps to the right, another "L" magically appeared. Moments later came the "I" and finally the big "E."

So maybe this wasn't as impressive as the Ohio script performed by the considerably bigger Ohio State University band, but they can't do their show inside. Our performance only took one rehearsal and a bit of creative choreography to chart the smooth transition from letter to letter. The result was a truly unique tribute to a very special person.

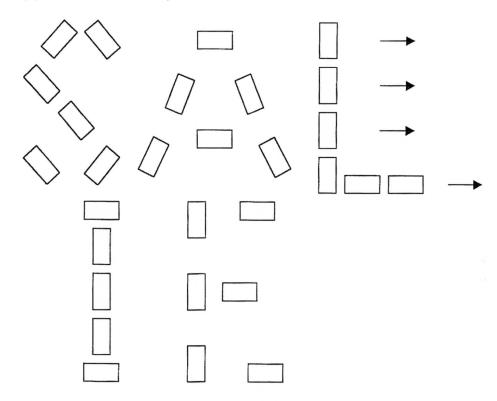

Library Association Meetings

Librarians like to get together as much as the next guy. We also really enjoy learning and sharing information; there are lots of local, state and national library-oriented meetings across the country. These conferences are not all work. There is usually time devoted to socializing, fun and frivolity. A library book cart drill team demonstration brings the learning, sharing and fun parts of a conference together in one event. How perfect.

There are a few challenges to pulling off a successful association presentation. You need to identify whether there is an area suitable for a performance. It must be large enough to wheel around all the carts, and with enough space for the throngs of people who will want to catch every move.

Finding an appropriate time to appear can also present some problems, since conferences are chock full of events. The best time to perform may be at the conclusion of a banquet meal, during the breaks or at the opening of a general meeting. Space constraints may make the first and last of these more difficult, but the audience will already be assembled. Drawing a crowd may be harder during session breaks, since people will be wandering in and out.

Performance time and location will probably be determined by the event organizers, who usually have a very full agenda and long "to do" lists. Contact them early and provide them with suggestions about times and locations where performances may be successful. Remember, they will probably need to have a thorough explanation of what a library book cart drill team is and why it should appear at the conference or meeting.

When the meeting is local, recruiting team members will probably be easier, especially if staff is already attending the conference. Think small. A group of only four or five can effectively demonstrate book cart drill teaming and be loads of fun. Keep the routine simple and it will be possible to draft and train a few new members to fill out the group if needed.

Corralling carts may be another challenge if the meeting is held outside a library. Even at meetings in a library, carts may not be readily available. Unless prior arrangements are made, most carts may well be holding a full load of books. (Imagine that!)

For other locations, try making arrangements with the host or closest library to borrow a few carts. Hopefully, they will have transportation for the carts, but be sure to check. If not, see if a team member has a van or truck available.

Coordinating all these special circumstances will be a challenge, but worth it. You may be preaching to the choir, but they will appreciate the message.

Community Events

Parades are the obvious venue for a library book cart drill team venturing out into the community, but there are a variety of other opportunities. Most of these will adapt well to a non-linear performance that uses a collection of stationary routines.

Fairs

Most country or city fairs provide a number of large and small stage events of all types. A library book cart drill team may not qualify as a headliner, but there will probably still be a great audience of families, kids and teens gathered around the smaller venues. In a stage performance, music can be highlighted, since a sound system will probably be available. A country theme, either in the music or using a square dance caller, seems most appropriate for a fair performance.

Almost any community event can be an opportunity to perform if there is a large flat area in which to maneuver. There are lots of possibilities, including street fairs, art festivals and ethnic celebrations. The list goes on and on. Check the local directories, papers and Chamber of Commerce for a list of events in your area. Contact the coordinators to learn more about the event; talk to others who have attended; and, if it looks promising, volunteer to perform.

School Functions

School assemblies and events are also great places to take a library book cart drill team. Check to see if the school hosts family after-school activities, such as "Communities in Schools" or similar programs. The school gym provides an excellent surface and a wide open space for maneuvering. The school library may even lend you their carts.

Kids are a great audience. They appreciate the act, and it's a wonderful way to encourage them to visit their public library and show them what a fun and inviting place it can be.

· 4 ·

Getting Ready to Roll:
Planning Your Performances

Get the Green Light

You're convinced. A book cart drill team is just what your library needs, but you've got some work to do. The job will be much easier once you have won over your director to the wonderful opportunities the drill team can bring your library.

Make sure that your administration is on board with your plan. You might want to write a memo to your director, asking for their support for the book cart drill team, explaining the cost and telling what steps you will be taking toward this new project. This is especially important if staff time will be used.

Even though this will be a fun project for library staff, friends and supporters, it will have some serious benefits to the library. Tell your administration about what you expect to accomplish with your book cart drill team. The memo should emphasize those benefits that are most appropriate for your situation, such as improving staff teamwork or reaching an under-served population. For example, your group may be planning to appear in an ethnic festival for a population targeted for library outreach.

There are several administrative decisions that will need to be made. Most of them involve money in one way or another. From the library's perspective, one of the main costs could be personnel if the participants will be paid for their work on the drill team. In many organizations, parade participation is voluntary, but this needs to be clearly established and spelled out from the beginning.

It is also important to determine if all the planning and other support participation will be done on work time, and what its impact might be. Special services, such as driving library vehicles for transporting carts, may need to be done by authorized personnel, and therefore may need to be done on work time.

Be sure to spell out any other costs that can be anticipated, such as entry fees and decorations. Let the administration know if there are alternative sources for funding, such as Friends groups, and how the bill paying will be accomplished.

This project will take some time to complete, and you will need support along the way. Keep them advised of your progress. From time to time, let everyone know what's been done and what is needed for the drill team. This helps to keep the administration a part of the plan.

Explain What a Book Cart Drill Team Is

"You want to do WHAT with our book carts?" Unless someone in your library has been lucky enough to see a live book cart drill team performance, you may have some trouble getting your colleagues to share your vision.

Talk to people. Explain your new idea. Your vivid description and enthusiasm will help them see the possibilities.

Write an article for your library's newsletter. Describe what a drill team is, what it does, and what the benefits would be. Keep it light-hearted and promote the benefit of your plan.

Photographs of other drill teams have appeared in some select publications. Post these on your staff and public bulletin boards. These may help the uninformed see what you have in mind.

If all else fails, show them. Be bold. Take a few minutes at your next general staff meeting, staff development day or Friends meeting to demonstrate. With a friend's help, work out a simple, two-cart routine that will so impress everyone they will wholeheartedly support the idea of a drill team.

Even if everyone doesn't completely understand what a book cart drill team is, they can share your enthusiasm for a new, unusual project.

Recruit as Many People as Possible

Now that everyone is impressed and enthusiastic about your terrific plan, there are some specific things you need to do to launch the drill team.

Recruiting volunteers is first. Those carts don't move by themselves. Get as many people as possible to volunteer. Drill teams can really be any size. You can perform with only four; but the more volunteers, the more fun and the more impressive your drill team will be.

See Chapter 5 for more tips on recruiting.

Find a Drill Sergeant

What's a drill team without a drill sergeant? You need someone to shepherd that herd of book carters, working with them, nurturing them, until that ungainly group emerges on parade day as a snappy precision unit. At least, that's the vision.

A good drill sergeant must have a vision, but must also be patient and gentle, willing to settle for a less-than-perfect group that's having a great time despite their flaws. The sergeant also needs to be prepared to walk backwards throughout most of the parade and to subsequently become acquainted with muscles previously unknown.

Hopefully, the drill sergeant will be able to attend all the rehearsals and parades. Since the leader position is critical, having a backup is a great idea. Each leader has his/her own style, so if there is a backup, have him/her work with the group in the rehearsals too.

Find Book Carts with Good Wheels

Every library has book carts; and just like drill team members, they seem to come in just about every shape and size imaginable. But they all have a few things in common. Each has four wheels, shelves, two ends—and a mind of its own.

Experience has taught us that the best carts to use have large, well-oiled wheels, a height that is comfortable for most people to push, and are as light a weight as possible. But you might just have to work with whatever you have. The bigger wheels are a definite benefit when it comes to negotiating obstacles like potholes and railroad tracks. Little wheels can be easily caught and cause the book cart to tip over.

Develop Spiffy Routines

The next step is to develop spiffy routines that fit your particular situation. In Chapters 6, 7, and 8 you will find several routines that have proven themselves over time. You may need to adapt them for your particular situation. Some routines work very well with just a few team members. If you have many volunteers, the more elaborate routines may be just what the team needs. Try out some simpler routines in the beginning. Then tackle those crowd-dazzling extravaganzas!

Secure Transportation for You and Your Carts

As much fun as pushing those book carts can be, that's not the ideal way to get them to the site of your drill team's performance.

For parades, be sure that transportation to both the start and finish of the parade have been well planned for both the drill team members and the book carts. Both people and book carts need to get there on time and in good condition.

Once the parade is over, those drill team members are going to need a rest. Make sure that someone is on hand to see them safely to their car or home.

If convenient, everyone might want to gather at the library or some other facility that has free parking for parade participants.

Gather Your Command Tools

Ever been to a quiet parade? Didn't think so. There are cheering crowds, blaring bands and all sorts of other noises. Library book cart drill teams make lots of noise as well, so it is essential for the leader to establish a means of communicating with all the members in the group. There are several options, including bullhorns, whistles and visual signals. The group will need to know what routine to do, when to start, and when to stop. Using a combination of the above may be the best choice for most groups.

Find Money (But You Won't Need Much)

Almost all projects require some money; but book cart drill teams can be a real bargain. Many of the potential expenses can be reduced or eliminated with a little creativity. In the following sections we'll offer some ideas to get you started on banners and decorations that are low-cost or practically free.

One small possible expense you may encounter is a parade entry fee. Of course, local parades are great places for the book cart drill team to perform, and many of them are so grateful to have such crowd-pleasing entertainment that they don't even charge entry fees. Some parades do charge a small entry fee, however, just as a way of ensuring that entries really do show up on parade day.

The fees are usually small, no more than fifty dollars, most of the time less than that.

At some parades, motorized entries are required to carry a special insurance policy that holds the parade, the city and the rest of those official types blameless if anything bad happens. If you use your library's bookmobile or delivery van, check with your administration about the needed insurance policy. They will be able to help with this type of special need.

Fly Your Flag: Get a Banner

Your parade entry should begin with a banner announcing to the world your precision book cart drill team. Not only does the banner identify your unit in a parade, it also promotes your library. After all, just who is sponsoring this terrific, entertaining drill team? The library or Friends group may already have a banner that would work. Or you might choose to have a banner professionally made, if the funds are available. Vinyl banners stand up to all types of weather and are lightweight and sturdy. This would cost around one hundred dollars, but can be used for several years.

You may decide to produce the banner in the most economical and fun way—you may want to make it a library or Friends craft project. A good size is thirty to thirty-six inches wide and six to ten feet long, with a sleeve running along the top of the banner. The sleeve is made to hold a supporting rod, which can be made of metal, PVC pipe or wood, and should be slightly longer than the banner. This gives the banner carriers something to hold on to.

Your parade banner can also be a billboard for communicating with your local community. If your library has an upcoming anniversary celebration, a special program to promote or a new campaign to launch, the banner leading your drill team is the perfect place to display the message.

The banner can be as elaborate or as simple as you choose. The simplest message would be the name of your library or other

A simple banner can be very effective (photograph by Judith Prowse Buskirk).

sponsoring group. A more elaborate message might remind voters about an upcoming bond election.

There are many messages in between that could use the good publicity that your drill team can generate. A special message banner can also serve as a second banner trailing behind the carts.

For extra fun, have the holders rotate the banner whenever the carts perform a circle maneuver.

Decorate Your Carts

Let's face it, library carts are not the most attractive things on four wheels. And chances are the carts that you use for the book cart drill team (especially if you are taking them out on the roadway) will not be your newest, but rather the old ones that may already have undergone welding surgery and other mechanical operations.

The library in Santa Cruz was lucky enough to have a collection of red carts, so they looked stunning right out of the gate. But if you are like us, you are stuck with exciting colors like putty. These carts could use some help.

You want to look good, or at least presentable. There are lots of little touches you can do to dress up your carts for the occasion. You can go for the uniform look and decorate each cart alike, or let your members express their own personality. If you go with the last option, try to have a similar theme or color scheme to tie the look together.

No matter how you decide to decorate your carts, the prime directive is to be certain that everything is well secured. It can be taped, bungeed, tied or Crazy Glued (not recommended), but be sure that it can withstand the rigors of the road. Carts glide smoothly on carpet but will shake, rattle and vibrate on pavement. If your beautiful decorations aren't well fastened, your cart may undress itself all along the parade route. A potentially shocking cart striptease may take place. This can be messy (we don't want to litter) and embarrassing if your cart ends up nude by parade's end. Both of these consequences could, but probably won't, be scandalous.

There are special occasion parades and festivals that present unique cart decorating opportunities.

Christmas

The Christmas season comes with tons of decoration options. The Lincoln Library in Springfield, Illinois, participates in a Christmas parade, and they deck their carts out appropriately. Individual expression is encouraged here, with each "Cart Wheeler" designing their creation. Their Christmas carts feature gold garland draping the sides, cut-out cardboard sleighs with big red bows on the fronts, wrapping paper covering the shelves and stuffed animals—

Top: The Lincoln Library Cart Wheelers decorate their carts and themselves to show their holiday spirit (photograph by Norman Langhoff). *Bottom:* Annette Hunsaker (right) and the rest of the Cart Wheelers from Lincoln Library are wearing the green for St. Patrick's Day (photograph by Julie Wullner).

from teddy bears to Big Bird—coming along for the ride. All the Cart Wheelers complete the festive look by donning Santa hats.

St. Patrick's Day

For St. Patrick's Day, the Cart Wheelers dropped the red decorations and decided to go for the green. Shamrocks of various sizes are taped all over the carts. They sport green and white pom-poms, streamers and balloons. Their leader, Annette Hunsaker, makes a great looking leprechaun.

Floral Parades

One major consideration is to check to see if there are any requirements for the parade or event. Floral parades in particular may require that a certain percentage of the "vehicle's" surface be adorned with the flower du jour.

Pierce County Library's versatile book cart saddles are an easy way to display flowers in Tacoma's Daffodil Parade (photograph by Lynne Zeiher).

For Pierce County, the flower du jour was the daffodil, since it was the Daffodil Festival. Our unit needed to display at least 1,000 of these bright yellow blossoms. In our first year we had each carter bring a basket, which we bungeed to the cart; and we made simple arrangements on top of each cart. They didn't look great— no self-respecting florist would have claimed these—even at the beginning of the parade—but they did the job.

The next year someone developed a really nifty idea that we have been able to reuse year after year. We cut runners out of clear plastic mesh sheets and draped them over the carts like a saddle. Each year we just insert flower stems into the holes in the mesh on both sides of the cart, tape down the sheet on the top and we're ready to roll. Beautiful, easy and cheap.

Faux Books Cart Decoration

Somehow a book cart just doesn't look right without books. But carrying a truckload of books during a parade is not only unwise, it could be a disaster. The cart would be too heavy and most of the books would end up littering the street as the rumbling of the carts shook them off.

But there is a way to have the look without the weight and mess. Terry Ford at Pierce County Library devised a plan to utilize wornout materials in the library to simulate a cart full of books. Using a block of old video boxes and the covers from discarded books, she made a shelf full of faux books. It takes some time to accumulate enough used materials and to put them all together, but the results are impressive and sturdy enough to last through many parade seasons.

Making a faux book shelf requires: twenty video boxes; forty book spines cut from book jackets, two long book jackets (for a two sided block), glue gun with glue sticks, staples, strapping tape, and fairly wide clear tape.

To make a block of video boxes:

A. Start by hot gluing the flat sides of the video boxes together. Be sure to keep the bottoms of the boxes even. The boxes should be the same height and depth. It works best to alternate the spine and the opening sides of the boxes when creating the block.

B. Secure the block of video boxes by wrapping the whole block

The tape holding the boxes together also serves as a good surface to apply glue for sticking on the covers.

with strapping tape. Two or three straps around will secure the block well and provide a surface for gluing the jacket.

C. For a truly festive look, we drilled holes in the tops of the video boxes to hold flowers.

Jean Flynn tests out the holes drilled to hold flowers during the parade.

To make the faux book covers:

A. Put aside those book jackets that are long enough to span the width of the video boxes plus an inch or two to wrap around the sides.

B. Cut the spines out of discarded book jackets. Keep the front covers for later.

C. Working from the spine on the long book jacket, staple the cut spines side by side until they cover the entire jacket. Place the staples at the top and bottom of the spines.

To assemble:

A. Fold the first spine over the edge of the video box block and secure it with hot glue and tape. Tape down the edges of the first and second spines along the fold. Be sure to align the bottom of the book jacket with the bottom of the block.

B. Hot glue the surface of the video box spines and or the strapping tape and begin laying down the book jacket as the glue is applied.

Sherry Norris hot glues a complete book jacket to the video boxes.

C. Fold the end of the jacket over the last video box and secure with tape and glue. Only about an inch or two needs to overlap at each end. The jacket can be trimmed if desired.

D. Run a long strip of wide clear tape down the middle of the faux spines to help them lay flat.

E. If the faux shelf will be visible from both sides, secure another adapted book jacket on the other side of the block.

F. Trim the fronts of two of the saved cut book jackets. Tape or glue them to the ends of each block.

G. Drill or punch a hole in the top of the block. Attach it to the book cart with a bungee cord around the cart handle. Alternately, bungee cords can be stretched vertically or horizontally over the block to attach it to the carts.

Signs

Fronts, back and sides of the cart can be used to show who you are or send a message. You might consider making a connection between the library and the parade's theme. In one parade the theme was "Romance in Bloom," so Pierce County toyed with the idea of displaying enlarged color photocopies from the covers of some bodice rippers on the fronts and backs of the carts. Covers from popular children's books or best sellers can also be eye catching and attractive.

If you use words on your signs, make them as large and few as possible. You will be a moving target, so you want the sign to be easy and quick to read from a distance. The crowd may have missed your banner, so it doesn't hurt to have your library's name on each cart. If you have a branch system, how about having the name of each of your branches on a cart.

One group put a single large letter on each cart and then spelled out simple phrases as they marched down the street. Even if you only have four carts, they could spell out R-E-A-D (or D-E-A-R if you get out of order). Either one is an appealing message.

Don't forget to put your signs on both ends of the carts. Spinning and turning maneuvers can make it hard to keep one side facing forward.

A reusable cart sign is easy to create by making a plastic saddle out of heavy-duty clear plastic. Make colorful paper signs with the Library's name or similar message, laminate them and tape one on each end of the saddle. At parade time drape the plastic "saddle" over the cart's midsection with the signs hanging over each side, and secure it to the top of the cart with tape. At the end of the parade remove the tape and fold up your saddle sign for the next time. Ride 'em cartboy. This signage works best on flat-topped carts.

If you are totally devoid of funds, consider finding a sponsor. Be like the bus companies and sell space on the side or front of your carts. A local bookstore, merchant or other company might be amenable to sponsoring your appearance for a bit of memorable PR. It can also be a noncommercial entity like your Friends group or Foundation.

Whatever the sign, be sure to laminate it in case of rain, puddles or other parade hazards. A good laminated sign will last parade after parade and is worth the investment.

Decorate Your People

Clothes make the man and go a long way to making a precision book cart drill team. Having everyone in your parade unit wear the same costume really classes up your drill team and makes everyone feel like part of the unit. But that can cost extra money. Not everyone can afford to buy all new duds for a special event; therefore, it works best to keep the outfit simple and utilize items of clothing that everyone is likely to have, such as blue jeans.

A basic uniform could be jeans and a white shirt; or you might choose a specific color of pants to be worn with the T-shirt from last summer's reading program. For a small amount of money you can design a "team" shirt, or a shirt with your library's logo. Use your imagination here and keep in mind the cost of uniforms and how much they are used. If your team plans to participate in several parades, buying a uniform may be more realistic.

Whatever uniform you select, make sure that the drill team members are comfortable. Dress for the weather you will be performing in. Keep in mind that it may feel chilly when you are waiting for the parade to start—but once those carts start rolling, you'll warm up quickly. We've had members stripping off their sweatshirts during the parade. This is a tricky move to make while pushing a cart, and perhaps not exactly the image desired. Outdoor practices can help you decide how to dress on parade day.

Hats can be a very practical addition to your uniform. They protect team members from the sun and even the rain. Remember sunscreen and drinking water, if you will be performing in the summer heat.

Be kind to your feet. The most important part of your uniform will be shoes. Definitely choose them for comfort. Asphalt roadways can get very hot in the summer. Comfortable walking shoes and socks are a necessity. The ever popular white tennis shoes usually work great.

Changing your shirt color, or adding a special hat, is a simple way to alter the drill team uniform to fit a special occasion. If your local parade has a special theme, adapt your uniform accordingly. For the daffodil parade, the team might wear yellow shirts; purple for a lilac festival; or red, white and blue for a Fourth of July parade. Santa hats are almost a must for Christmas parades.

Find a Time and Place to Rehearse

Those spiffy routines that you have chosen for the drill team will require some practice. At first, a large room may offer plenty of space for learning the routines. Walking through the maneuvers without those pesky book carts is a good way to learn the basic moves. When the team graduates to using the book carts, a much larger space is needed. A parking lot (before or after business hours), or an alleyway or a driveway that can be blocked off for practice time, would offer the space that the team needs to perfect their routines.

It really helps if there is enough room for the entire routine to be completed by the whole team without having to stop in the middle. The amount of room needed depends on the size of your carts, the number of drill team members and the routines that you will be practicing.

Make It Fun

Remember your sales pitch. You promised that the recruits would have a good time. Do everything you can to make sure that this happens. Be ready to laugh. Keep the tone of your rehearsals and performances light. Have a smile at the ready. The up-beat attitude that you have going into this project will pay off later.

Sure, pushing a book cart through these spiffy routines looks easy on paper. But it's not all that easy to get a group of novices all going in the right direction at the right time. Sometimes it will seem like you are attending your very first dance class. Don't worry; you won't step on anyone's feet this time, and hopefully your cart won't roll over anyone either.

But those book carts don't always do what they're told. Mistakes will happen. That's part of the fun that everyone will have even during the parade itself. Someone is bound to zig when s/he should have zagged. Laugh and the crowd will laugh with you.

Remember that part of the goal is to show the public that librarians don't live in ivory towers. They, we, are just folks, friendly, fun loving folks. No one on your team is an expert; everyone is learning something new and will appreciate patience, encouragement and a good laugh along the way.

Don't Take Yourselves Too Seriously

Through rehearsals and performances, always keep the tone light. The best way to ensure that everyone on the team has a good time is to make sure that no one takes this project too seriously. There will be no test; this is the time for people to work together, to laugh and have a good time while promoting your library.

No one on the team needs to worry about not doing a good job. Remind them frequently that miscues are as much fun, if not more fun, than getting everything right. Relax and enjoy.

Remember the military color guard that always leads the parade? Remember how those soldiers walk—shoulder to shoulder, always in step, without once looking at their feet? Do they look like they are having fun? No way, man. Well, make up your mind that the book cart drill team will never look like that. Just how dignified can you be while pushing a rattling book cart down the street? The very idea brings a smile. And that's the whole idea—to bring a smile, to the people lining the parade route, and especially to those wonderful people who have volunteered to be part of this team.

Add Your Bookmobile

If your library has a brightly decorated bookmobile or delivery van, include it in your parade entry. Not only is it familiar to your community, it also serves as a big billboard, reminding everyone who you are.

The bookmobile can also be an emergency rescue vehicle—just in case a cart or drill team member needs help during the parade. Those pesky emergencies are hard to handle along the parade route. Being able to load a broken cart, or a distressed team member, into the bookmobile can save the day for everyone. It is also handy for carrying those items that are handy to have before and after—but not during—the parade, like handbags, water bottles and jackets.

Put the bookmobile behind the book carts in your parade unit. Use your bookmobile or delivery van to keep the unit behind you from intruding on your "stage." Include the bookmobile driver in your practices, or at least give them an idea of what to expect. Then they will know how much room those dazzling routines require and can use the bookmobile to guarantee you the space you need.

· 5 ·

Getting Into the Act:
Recruiting Team Members

A book cart drill team takes lots of planning. Once the plan is in place, it's time to start recruiting drill team members.

"You Want Me to Do What?"

As the drill team organizer, you've had to be a good salesman. You have already sold your idea to your library administration. Now put those skills to work recruiting team members. Don't be discouraged if the first people you approach turn you down. They just don't know how much fun they will miss.

And it will be fun. Trust us. It really is. Organizing the team is hard work. But when the team starts practicing and performing, everyone really does have a good time. How can you miss? The people who agree to join this project will already be primed to have fun.

Be Enthusiastic

Enthusiasm is contagious, and your attitude toward this project will carry you far. Everyone wants to be part of a winning project; and that's exactly what the book cart drill team is.

A Picture Is Worth a Thousand Words

If you need some help convincing those reluctant recruits, show them this book. Just take a look at the pictures of those successful drill teams. Those happy faces will surely convince the most hesitant prospects.

The More the Merrier—Recruit Everyone

As you meet and talk with people, consider recruiting them for the drill team. Although you can have a very good book cart drill team with as few as six to eight, the more people involved, the more fun everyone will have.

Staff

Start with your fellow staff members. Ask everyone. Invite them to join this wacky project. Even the shy, quiet person you hardly ever see may turn out to be one of the most excited drill team members.

Use e-mail, the telephone, your in-house newsletter, every means possible to recruit staff members. Put up a poster in the staff room. Use a few minutes at staff meetings to recruit drill team members. Show them the pictures in this book. Get a buddy to help you give a live demonstration. Your enthusiasm will draw more people to this project.

Staff Family Members

After recruiting from within your staff, look outward for more able bodies. The family members of your staff have an interest in the library. Capitalize on this. Invite them to join the drill team. This is just the kind of project that may even appeal to those aloof, sophisticated teens. Spouses and kids make great banner carriers, since no rehearsal time is required.

Friends of the Library

Don't forget those kind and generous people who run the book sales and have probably helped raise money for the drill team. The local Friends group already are enthusiastic library supporters. Their spouses and children just might join the drill team, too. Even if the Friends don't participate in the parade itself, they can increase team morale by volunteering to pay for everyone's lunch after the big performance. It's a great way to say "thanks for a job well done" and to encourage future parade participation.

Your Favorite Patrons

We all have favorite patrons, those people you look forward to talking with every time they visit the library. Ask them to participate in the drill team. Show them that it really is their library. And let them share a good time with the library staff that serves them.

And remember, you need to recruit support people as well as actual marchers—so don't let those behind-the-scenes types get away. A successful book cart drill team requires support and work from many people. There are plenty of jobs to go around.

The Marching Unit

The core of the drill team will be those courageous souls who agree to maneuver the book carts. Although this is not a difficult job, it does require a pleasant disposition and some stamina.

The other major requirement for a book carter is time. It does take some time to learn those spiffy routines, and to practice them. Getting those book carts to behave properly does take some practice.

Time to attend performances is a must. That's the whole point of the drill team—to perform. Although parades don't take much time themselves, it does take time to get ready and find your place in the line-up. Many parades require participants to be in place an hour or more before the parade starts. When the parade is over, it takes a little bit of time to round up the carts and transport team members to their cars or homes.

Even though we stress how much fun the book cart drill team is, there is still hard work involved. When recruiting team members, make sure they understand exactly what will be expected of them. Get them to commit to rehearsals and performances. If someone has shown up for every practice but misses the performance, they leave a big hole in the team that is very hard to fill.

Having alternates lined up is a good backup plan. Illness or other emergencies can keep team members from showing up on parade day. It's best to heed the Scouts' motto and be prepared. This makes the big day less stressful for everyone involved in the team.

Behind the Scenes Jobs

Those book carters may have the glamorous jobs, but many people are needed behind the scenes to help ensure that the team has a successful performance.

If there are enough volunteers, each of these behind-the-scenes jobs can be assigned to a different person. However, if necessary, one or two people can wear these different hats.

Decision-Makers

Just where is the book cart drill team going to appear? Is there a special event that they want to participate in? Or are there several local parades that the team can choose from? The decision needs to be made. The drill team members may decide, or a volunteer may plan the appearances, with input from the drill team, the administration, the staff and the local Friends group.

One hurdle to overcome may be in discovering the possibilities. The local visitors and convention bureau can help. They often have a listing of the parades and special events in the area. Individual cities also have contact information for parades within their jurisdiction. This is also the time to use those contacts at local organizations. For example, the local Shrine members participate in many parades and will share their knowledge of local parade schedules.

Parade or Event Liaison

Parades just don't happen, they require a great deal of planning. In even the smallest community there is some type of parade application process. This may be nothing more than a way of getting information about the entry for the parade announcer. In larger parades this may truly be an application: Not everyone who applies will be invited to participate in the parade. Participants are usually required to sign a waiver that says that the parade organizers will not be held responsible for damages or injuries to participants.

Each parade may have rules regarding the conduct of participants. For safety reasons, many parades now prohibit throwing candy or other material during the parade. These rules of conduct must be passed along to each of the book carters and all others involved in the team.

(See Appendix A for sample parade applications and rules.)

Whatever the application process, someone has to do the paperwork. The parade organizers will need to have the name and telephone number of one person that they can contact with questions or with changes in parade plans. This person will be given all of the information about where the drill team needs to be, when they need to be there, how the parade will progress and where the parade ends. It is essential that all of the information is collected and shared with everyone involved.

Communicator

All of this vital information has been collected. Someone needs to assume responsibility for passing it along and for organizing the team's appearance.

Each team member needs to know what is expected of him or her. Where will the team meet? When? Will transportation be provided from some central point to the start of the parade? Is everyone responsible for his or her own transportation? Some participants may need maps to the staging area.

How will the team members get from the end of the parade back to the starting point, or back to their transportation? It is also very important to know exactly who will be participating in each performance, so that the correct number of carts can be brought to the staging area. Having too many or too few carts can cause a problem. A big part of the communicator's job is to not just inform participants about the event details but to get commitments concerning who will be in each parade. The larger the library system and drill team size, the bigger and more important this job is.

The communicator also needs to be sure all supplies, banners, decorations, and so forth, are gathered together and make their way to the parade. The communicator may also need to make the arrangements for the transportation of the carts themselves.

Having these issues managed by one person helps eliminate confusion and make the whole experience more pleasant for everyone. The person chosen for this job should have good organizational and communication skills.

Financier

Many good plans have dissolved because they lacked financial support. Even the smallest drill team needs to consider the importance of a financial planner.

First, what are the costs involved in preparing the book carts and the book carters? Materials for preparing the carts, decorating the carts and outfitting the team members may be needed. The financier can check to see if supplies can be purchased where the library has an account or arrange for individuals to be reimbursed for appropriate expenses.

Second, what are the costs of participating in the local event?

Does the parade/event require an entry fee? If the answer is yes, a check will need to be written by the Library or a supporting group, such as the Friends. Do the parade organizers require proof of insurance? The Library's business office or officer may need to contact the insurance agency to secure the appropriate certificate of coverage.

Third, each event may have transportation costs. Can a library vehicle be used to haul book carts and team members to the event? Who pays the costs?

The financier needs to determine how much money will be needed and the possible sources of income. Libraries may have special funds that can be used for most of the costs. The local Friends groups often have money for special projects. And there are always those fabulous bake sales!

Transportation Coordinators

If the drill team is performing anyplace outside of your library, you'll need some help getting people and book carts there. Because they are tools of our trade, book carts will be scattered all around your library. Brand one for each drill team member, plus an extra one just in case there's a major breakdown on parade day. If you don't have enough carts, don't be afraid to borrow from another branch or nearby library.

Have one or two people responsible for rounding up the carts the drill team will use. Gather them in one location, a place easily accessible to whoever will be transporting them to the parade or performance. This should be done the day before. Don't wait until the last minute. Ask staff to have the carts empty and ready for collection. One last inspection of wheels and they will be ready to load.

On parade day, book carts and drill team members will need to get to the start of the parade route. You'll need people to plan for the hauling of the carts and for organizing car pools or other transportation of drill team members.

Unless the parade route makes a complete circle, you will also need to have someone pick up the carts and tired drill team members. Make sure the transporters know where the parade starts, what route it takes, and where it ends. Because they will be driving a fairly large vehicle, have them scope out a good drop off point and a good spot to pick up the book carts.

Creative Types

Book cart drill teams need those folks whose talents include putting two or more colors together in eye-catching and pleasing designs.

Cart decoraters are very important. Three-tiered, putty-colored steel book carts are not particularly interesting to look at; in fact, they are pretty boring. They really need some sprucing up for parades. Enlist the help of artistic library staff to magically transform plain book carts into mini-floats. Give them a copy of the parade requirements, and then stand back.

Banner creators are needed too. A banner announcing your drill team is a must for parades. There are two basic options. The first is to have the banner commercially produced. Ask staff members with artistic skills to work with the company to design just the right banner.

The second option is to enlist staff members to create a banner. This is definitely less expensive. For Yakima, it was also a way to involve many staff members who would not have otherwise participated in the drill team.

More Marchers—Ahead of, Beside and Behind the Team

Some people might love to be part of the drill team but just don't have the time to learn the routines and attend practices. Don't let them get away—there are jobs for them, too.

Banner Carriers

Ask two of these ambitious people to carry the banner. They will truly be "team leaders," introducing the drill team and helping to set the pace. It would be a good idea for them to at least watch one rehearsal so they know how fast the team moves and how much room the routines take. You don't want the banner too far ahead of the drill team; and they will need to allow enough room for the routines.

Crowd Pleasers

Some parades allow participants to distribute things to on-lookers. Check the rules for the parade that you will be in. If the parade rules permit it, this is another way to put those ambitious people to work. They can march with the drill team and hand out candy, bookmarks or other library promotional materials. Here's a chance for your library to personally contact people in your community.

Book Clappers

If there are people in the group who want to march but not practice, the book clapper role will give them an activity that will be unexpected, eye-catching and amusing. The book clappers walk along with the carters, spinning and making noise with easy to make parade accessories, also called book clappers. Basically, a book clapping apparatus is a book that has lost its guts but gained a handle. (See Appendix B.)

DJs or Drummers

What's a parade without big bands and snappy marching tunes. Music adds bounce and excitement to a presentation, but may be difficult to hear above the cart roar in a normal parade. Still, there are some options worth considering.

If using music, the easiest method is to prerecord a song or medley of tunes on a cassette tape. The library's media department or group's DJ should fill both sides of the tape with the desired

In addition to escorting the boom box, the Pierce County Library DJs (Barbara Harris and Estelle Budne) also doubled as cheerleaders (photograph by Peter Sabin).

musical selections, so silent rewinding segments can be avoided. Some songs that groups have utilized include "Nine to Five" and "Marion the Librarian" from *The Music Man*.

A portable boom box, sufficiently secured to a cart via bungee cords or the like, can be pushed along the parade route by the book cart drill team's DJ. Go for the boom from the box—maximize the volume—or the melody may be drowned out by the carts. Don't count on the team being able to hear the music during the parade, especially if the music cart is in front of the unit. But for the audience to hear the music, the front of the unit is the best spot for it.

For stage presentations, a DJ to start and stop the music is pretty much essential—unless the tape is timed with a delay to allow a participant to turn it on and still make it back to the cart before the music starts. Either way, it's an easy task. Even a rocket scientist can do it.

Another way to make a noise in the parade is to develop a simple chant or prerecord one using that old favorite, the boom box. The Grace A. Dow Memorial Library Book Cart Drill Team in Midland, Michigan, has used a modified version of Garrison Keillor's library chant. (Look this chart up on the Prairie Home Companion web site, http://prairiehome.org; it's in the performance archive for December 13, 1997.) The DJ (or another poetic type) might want to compose a chant specifically for the group. The old military "sound off" beat can provide a workable cadence. Keep it simple and short, or prerecord it. Even just the name of the Library shouted to a specified beat can be effective.

Here's the chant that we have used:

PIERCE COUNTY (two claps) LI-BRA-RY (two claps)—*Repeat*
IMAGINATION (three claps) INFORMATION (three claps)
    Repeat

For a place that's in the know
PCL is where to go

Information A to Z
Knowledge is our specialty

In our branches you will find
We are here to serve your mind

We're the friendly library
Here in your community

PCL is where to go
For the place that's in the know
IMAGINATION (three claps) INFORMATION (three claps)
    Repeat
PIERCE COUNTY (two claps) LI-BRA-RY (two claps)—*Repeat*

Whatever the chant may be, the group may have trouble hearing each other if the line is long. Try reforming into a more compact unit. Have four shorter lines rather than one or two long lines. This will make it easier to stay in sync.

Keeping the marchers on-beat is aided by the use of a drum and drummer. Of course, it's essential that someone in the group actually owns a drum, since it's unlikely the purchase of a new one would be worth the investment. In addition, the drummer needs a good sense of rhythm, or things could run amuck rather than gain precision. On the positive side, if both these elements are available, a good drum rap will certainly be heard and add a steady accompaniment for the marchers.

If the group doesn't have a DJ or drummer, there is always the possibility that a marching band or dance team will be close by, providing some welcome music.

· 6 ·

Your Marching Orders: Choosing Routines

Everything is in place. The volunteers are ready and the book carts are waiting. All they need are marching orders. What kind of moves should you do to really impress the crowds? Here are some things to consider when you select the routines that will wow your audiences.

First, get to know the terrain. Take a few minutes to consider the physical conditions of your performance area. Parades usually follow main streets. You may think you know them well; after all, you may drive them daily; however, pushing a cart down those same streets may be a very different matter.

If there is time before the parade, even on parade day itself, the leader should try walking the route. Watch for terrain that might cause trouble, as well as choice spots to perform. Usually the leader will be continually selecting routines as the parade progresses. To make this even more challenging, he or she will be marching backwards. Hence, some advanced knowledge of the area is very helpful.

When selecting which routines to use, consider how wide the streets are. Some routines, such as the Spoke, require a wide space to perform. Will there be enough room? If the streets are wide and the drill team is small, a widely spread formation may be visually lost against the backdrop of the crowd. Choose routines that keep members closer together most of the time. This will make the members look like one unit, not scattered parts.

Look for hills, however small. They present unique problems. Book carts can suddenly change direction on unsuspecting drill team members. Simple, forward motion routines may be the best choice. If the hill is steep, simply pushing the book carts up the hill in a basic formation is probably the way to go. It's amazing how much heavier the carts are when you push them uphill. Definitely don't try any routines where you temporarily let go of the cart, such as spins and passes. Gravity may take control of the cart and send it off on its own.

Plan for other road hazards, like railroad tracks, curves and turns. Book carts need to meet railroad tracks squarely. If not, those pesky wheels may drop into the grooves of the tracks and can tip both cart and drill team member. Curves and turns are not the best places to perform those intricate routines. Choose a simple, basic formation for this section of the parade route. Remember, those on the outside of the curve must work much harder than those on the inside of the curve.

If the drill team will be performing indoors, find out exactly how much space there will be. Hopefully, you can practice in the room you will perform in. If not, lay out the dimensions in a larger space and practice your routines.

Have a plan, but be prepared to work out some kinks in rehearsals. What looks good on paper may not work out quite like you think. It takes a bit of work to establish the timing for many of the routines, such as cart passes, etc. Stay flexible during rehearsals and always be open to suggestions from all drill team members. They can really help work out problems. That also makes this a real team effort.

There are two basic types of moves: advancing and stationary. You'll want both types in your repertoire. Naturally, most of the time, parades move smoothly along their course. Those advancing routines are just the ticket. But be prepared for those small glitches most parades experience from time to time when the entire parade comes to a halt. Stationary routines are a must for these situations. Also, almost every parade has a review stand location where the group can really show off their stuff. This is a great location to initiate a stationary routine, since often there will be an announcer or MC who will be talking about your group as you perform. Hog the spotlight as long as possible with a great routine, such as the Pinwheel or Spoke. There may also be parade judges here.

Naming the routines selected for the drill team will accomplish two things. First, names can bring a chuckle and enhance the fun the team will have performing them. Second, funny names are much easier to remember. You might ask the team if they have any suggestions for routine names. It's a great way to enhance the fun and help everyone remember the routines.

To help make the drill team more successful and enjoyable, limit the number of routines in your group's repertoire, especially the first year. One stationary routine and three or four advancing routines should be enough for most parades. After the team has perfected those, start adding new ones. If you add a new routine or two each year, it can keep it fresh for the parade alumni.

While the team is learning those new routines—*and* on parade day—remember: Don't expect perfection. There are going to be mistakes, but that can be fun too. If everyone can laugh and move on, the experience will be more enjoyable for the whole drill team, and for your audience. That is the ultimate goal—for everyone to relax, have fun together and entertain the audience.

· 7 ·

Forward March!
Forward-Progress Routines

Most of the time in a parade the book cart drill team will be making tracks down the road. In small-town parades especially, there are often groups of people, such as political candidates, who are there just to be seen, so they simply stroll down the street. This is fine, but not very memorable. It is possible to just push book carts along the parade route, and this in itself will be interesting and different.

If the idea is to make a lasting impression, however, there are numerous simple routines that a group can master in only a few rehearsals. Performing a few of these maneuvers will really make the parade appearance worthwhile, both for the audience and the library.

The audience's immediate positive responses will psyche up the drill teamers, and the memory of the library's participation will stay with the crowd long after the parade is over.

But first, start your team off with a simple basic formation—a line. The line or lines can march parallel or perpendicular to the curb. The best basic formation for your group will probably be determined by its size.

SINGLE VERTICAL FILE

Smaller groups usually choose to march in single file down the street. It's the most versatile formation. The only trick is to keep from running over the heels of the person in front.

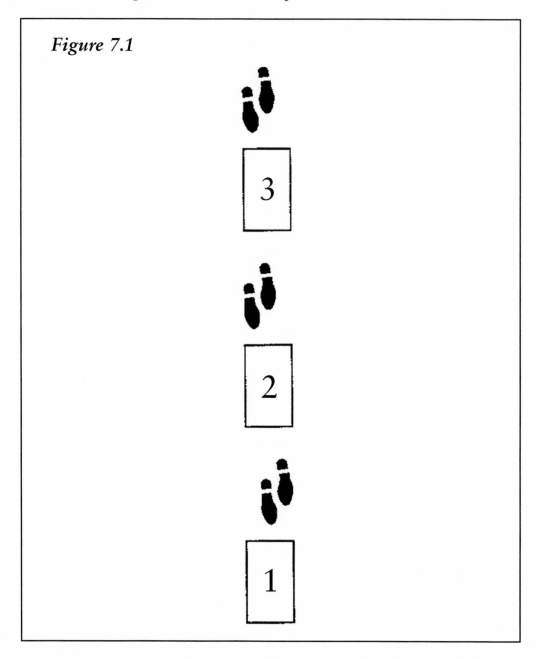

Figure 7.1

DOUBLE VERTICAL FILE

If there are enough people in the group, a double line looks more impressive. Even a small group of four can alternate between single file and a double line formation. It's also more fun for the marchers to be in pairs. Most of the routines in this book begin with the double line formation.

If you have a large group, consider adding even more vertical lines. Groups with lots of carts can opt to form three or four lines and still look good. This type of compact formation works great in situations where the group needs to be able to hear one another, such as when reciting the library's chant.

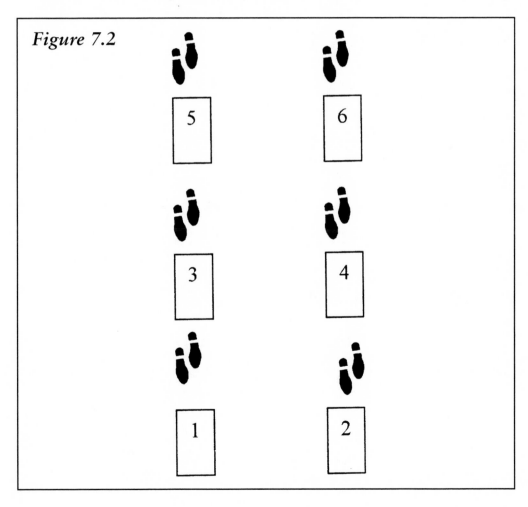

Figure 7.2

VERTICAL CHANGE NO. 1:
ONE LINE TO TWO

There are a couple of reasons that the group might want to change the basic marching formation. If there are only four to six carts, the group will look bigger if marching in single file most of the time; however, to perform many of the routines the group needs to start from a double line formation. Just changing formations can look pretty spiffy.

Changing from one line to two is a very simple maneuver. Every other person, starting with the second cart in line, angles out to the left side.

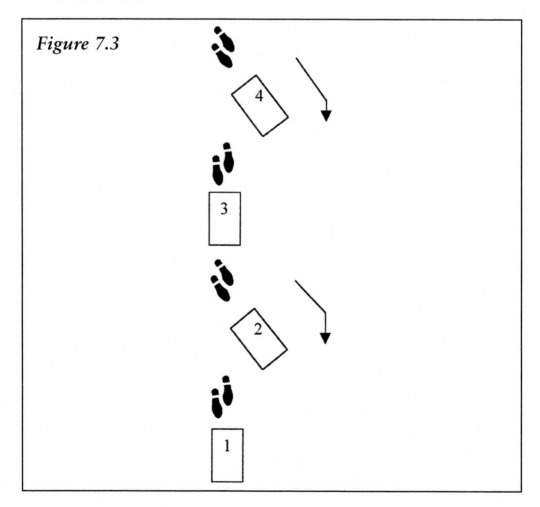

Figure 7.3

After moving out to the side, these carts head forward and pull up even with the cart that was previously in front. These even numbered carts need to pick up their pace a bit, while the odd numbered carts slow down some to allow the others to catch up with them.

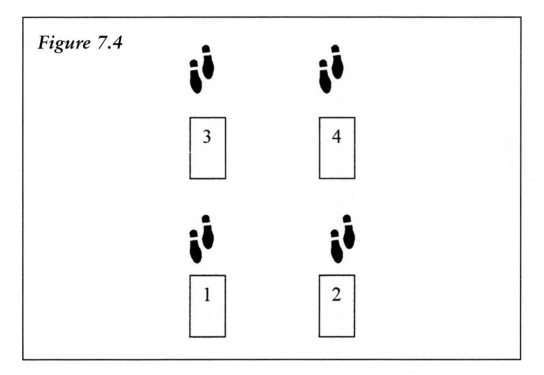

Figure 7.4

VERTICAL CHANGE NO. 2: TWO LINES TO FOUR

If the group is large enough to utilize a double line formation for most of the parade, there may be times when converting into four lines is desirable. When a double line has six or more people in it, there will be a long distance between the front and back of the line, and it is impossible for the back to hear the front. If the group has any type of chant, the more compact formation of four lines will make it easier for everyone to hear and thus stay in sync.

The conversion to four lines is the same as changing from one to two lines. The easiest way to form four lines is to have every other pair move out toward the curb.

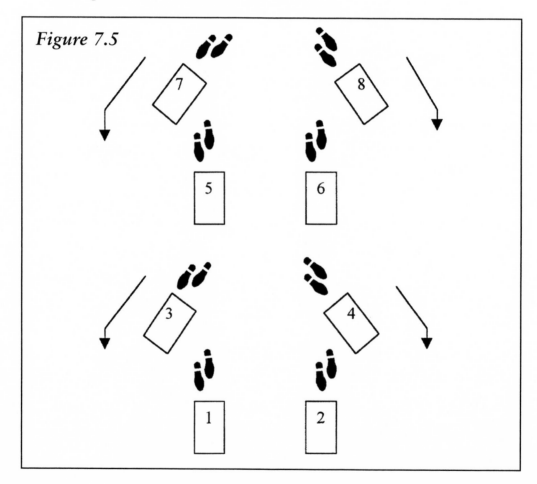

Figure 7.5

Again, it is important for the carts moving out to speed up and the others to slow down until the new formation is complete.

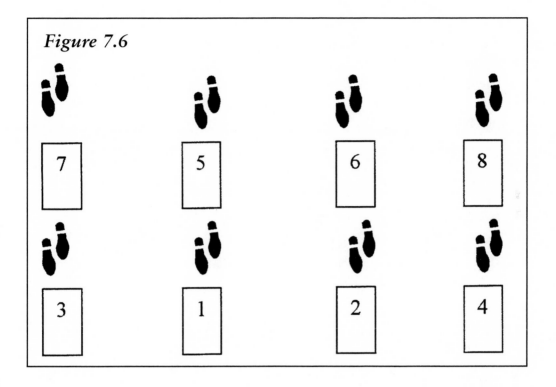

Figure 7.6

VERTICAL CHANGE NO. 3:
FOUR LINES TO TWO

When ready to return to the basic double line formation, signal for the regular front pair to pull forward while the pair behind them slows down to allow room for the outside pair to return to their original place. It is important for the line to keep moving forward so that room can be made for each cart to return to the original lines.

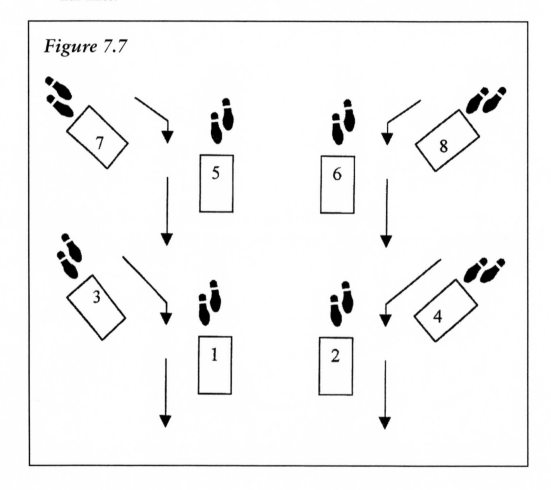

Figure 7.7

HORIZONTAL LINE

There have been groups that prefer to march in a line that runs from curb to curb. The St. Joseph County Library in South Bend, Indiana, marched abreast down the street because they used their carts to spell out different phrases. Each cart had a letter on the front of it. Periodically they would scramble around and spell out a new phrase, such as "Read More."

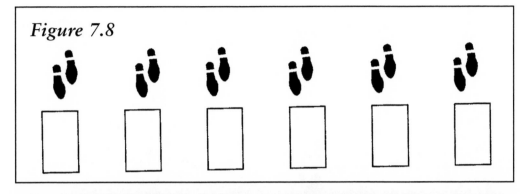

Figure 7.8

The Flathead County Library Truckers fill the streets of Montana with their horizontal formation (photograph by Thomas E. Laird).

It is important to preview the parade route when using the horizontal formation, in case the street width changes. Make sure there is enough room for all carts throughout the parade. If there are sections of the street that narrow, consider adjusting into a "V" formation (which I like to call the Flying Goose) so there is room for everyone.

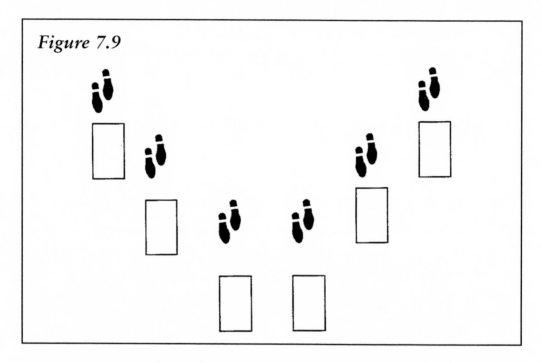

Figure 7.9

Another excellent trick is to change from vertical to horizontal and back. Switching from a parallel line to a perpendicular formation, or vice versa, is an impressive maneuver in itself. It also gives the group a larger repertoire of routines to do.

FAN OUT

Fan Out is a simple maneuver that makes your group look bigger by filling the street horizontally rather than vertically. It is also a starting step to the Spoke Routine. Here are the steps:

1. Front two carts begin the maneuver by moving forward but angling out toward the curbs in opposite directions. Other carts continue to move forward, speeding up their pace.

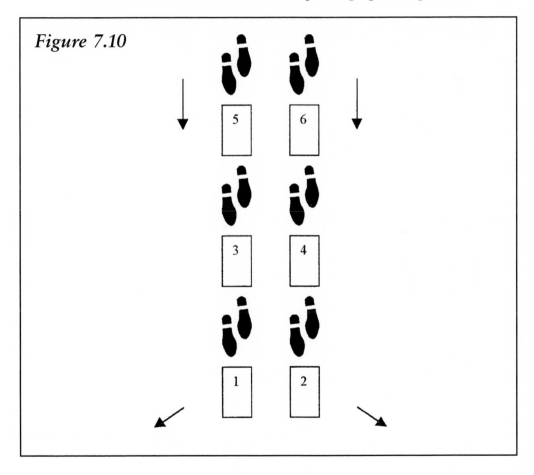

Figure 7.10

2. As 3 and 4 move forward, they begin to angle out, following the lead of 1 and 2, moving along beside them. 1 and 2 continue to move out toward the curbs. Continue until everyone is in one line, perpendicular to the curb and marching forward.

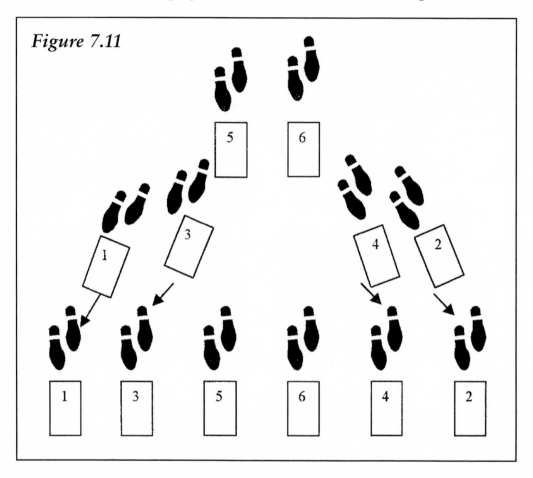

Figure 7.11

FAN IN

The Fan In routine is used to convert from a horizontal formation back to a two line vertical formation. The center pair in the line needs to march in place while each consecutive pair begins to move forward and in toward the center.

As each pair reaches the center, they should also march in place until both lines have been completely formed.

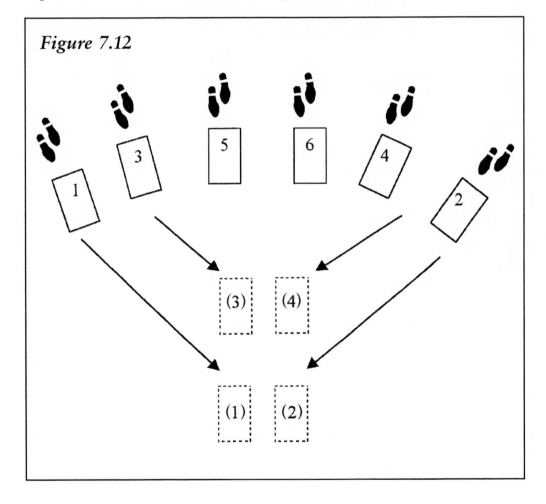

Figure 7.12

CROSSOVER VARIATIONS NO. 1: BASIC SINGLE

There are several variations of the crossover maneuver. If you plan on using more than one version, give each one a different name to avoid confusion.

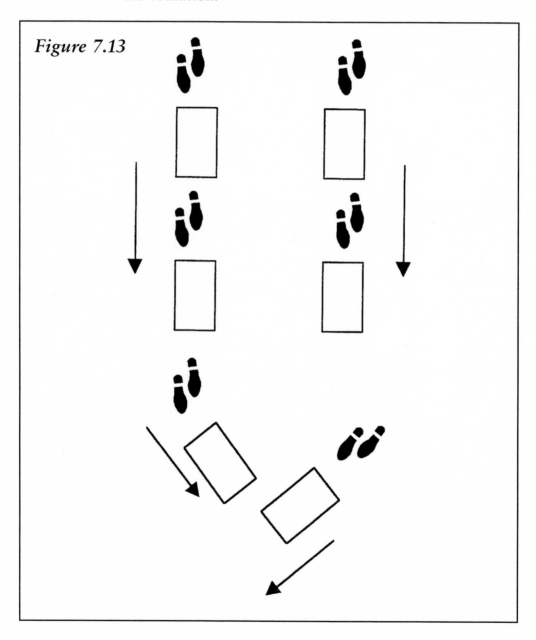

Figure 7.13

The basic plan is for each pair of carts to exchange places by crossing in front of each other while also continuing to advance forward. It is important to determine who is crossing over in front. It should either always be the same person (the odd or even numbered carts) going first OR whomever is on the right or left. If it isn't consistent, the crisscross can quickly become crash, crunch and chaos. It will be time to call in the tow truck to clear up the cart wreckage. Before concluding the maneuver, be sure everyone is back in their original positions.

In the Basic Single, only one pair of carts at a time crosses over. As soon as the first cart has completed the exchange, the next set begins the move. All the carts continue to march forward as the pairs cross. As soon as the end pair has completed their first cross, a signal is given for the front couple to cross over again, allowing everyone to return to their original position.

CROSSOVER VARIATION NO. 2: WEAVE

In this version, all the pairs cross over at the same time. For a precision look, wait until each pair has completed the first exchange before signaling the next cross over. Often the pairs farther down the line will be a few beats off the front. This method also makes it easier to assure that everyone ends up on his or her original side.

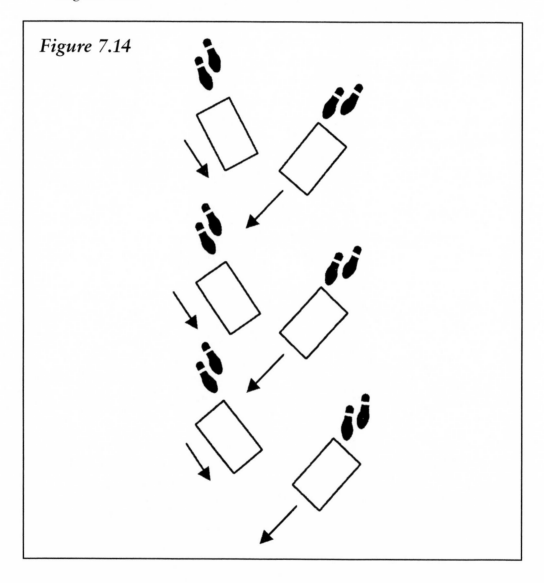

Figure 7.14

Members of the first Pierce County Library book cart drill team (DiAnne Sabin and Terry Ford) demonstrate the beginning steps of the "Weave" (photograph by Peter Sabin).

CROSSOVER VARIATION NO. 3: FLOURISH

To create a more weaving motion, let each pair continue crossing over again and again at their own pace. In this version the cart pushers need to be responsible for correctly realigning themselves at the end of the maneuver. For this reason, everyone may not finish exactly at the same time, but that's no big deal.

Try not to spread too far apart after each exchange. If the pair of carts create a wider and wider distance between themselves, it takes longer to complete the crossover and can begin to look pretty sloppy. Don't worry if an occasional crash occurs. Tow trucks really won't be necessary. Just laugh it off and keep going.

If you want to bring some flair to the standard weave or figure eight, add an opposite direction spin at the outside edge turns. It takes a bit more practice, but the results can be stunning.

After the carts have crossed in the middle and reached the outside, each cart should turn around in a complete circle instead of making a right angle turn.

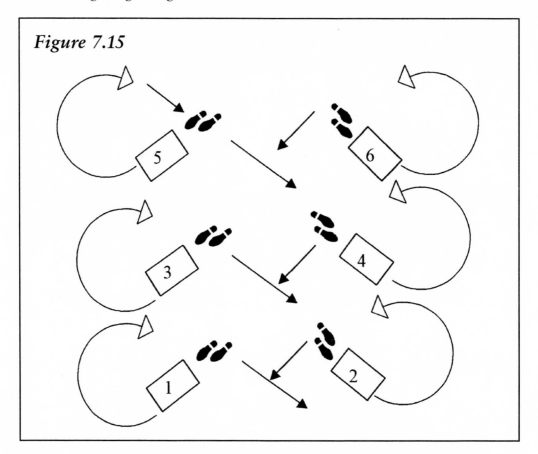

Figure 7.15

CROSSOVER VARIATION NO. 4:
X MARKS THE SPOT

This weaving move covers the entire street. Like the crisscross, it starts with two lines, the front pair crossing in front of each other. But instead of turning back after the cross, they continue on to the edge of the street. Each pair continues moving straight until they reach the front of the line, where the leader stands marking the crossing position.

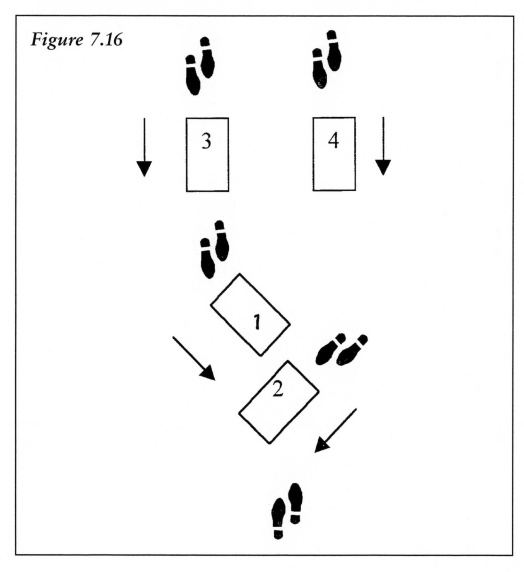

Figure 7.16

After crossing, each cart follows the one in front of them.

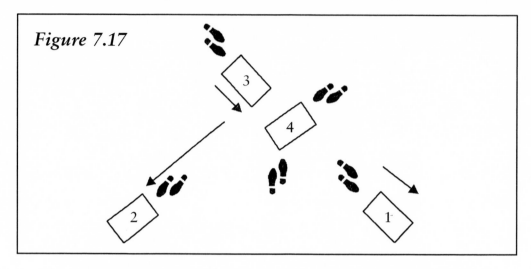

Figure 7.17

When the first cart gets to the curb, the carter makes a right angle turn and heads back toward the center of the street. Pairs should try to make turns at the same time and at points directly opposite each other. Each cart turns at this same spot.

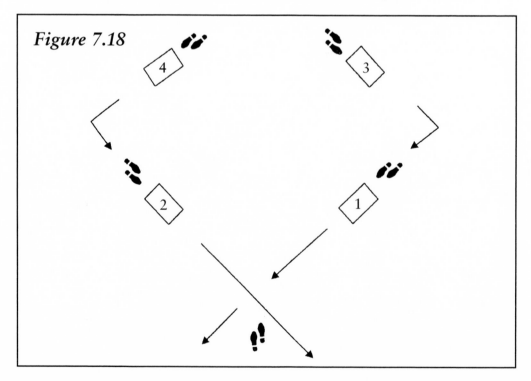

Figure 7.18

Carts continue to cross the street in a diagonal line and pass each other in the center of the street at a spot marked by the leader. The leader will need to hustle ahead to the new crossover spot as soon as the last cart has made their center pass.

CROSSOVER VARIATION NO. 6: CART PASS

This simple routine can be very impressive. It's also very versatile because it can be done while moving forward or when the parade has stopped. The only tricky part is to make sure the same person always passes the cart in front. Do this and every pass will be successful.

1. Start from a double line formation, with the lines fairly close together. At the signal, everyone turns their carts so that the wide sides are heading forward and are held by each end.

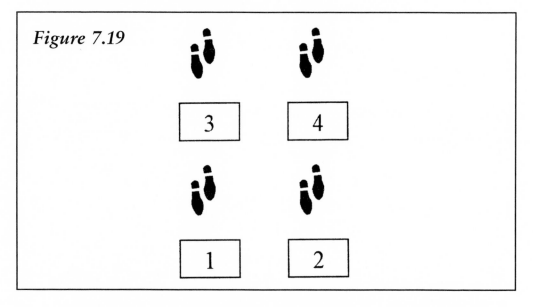

Figure 7.19

2. At the next signal, odd numbered carts are pushed forward and to the left, while even numbered ones are pushed to the right. Passing will go smoother if the odd numbered people push with the right hand and release the left hand. Use the free left hand to grab and guide the other cart during the pass. Even numbered person releases his cart as soon as his partner grabs it, and then reaches for the other cart. (Note: The drawing only demonstrates the move using carts 1 and 2. All the carts in the line execute the maneuver at the same time.)

After a few practices, this move will go smoothly. Partners

develop their own rhythm and technique. The leader should watch the passes to be sure everyone has completed the pass before signaling a second pass. Be sure to do an even number of passes so each person ends up with their own cart. At the end, don't forget to signal turning the carts back to their normal pushing position.

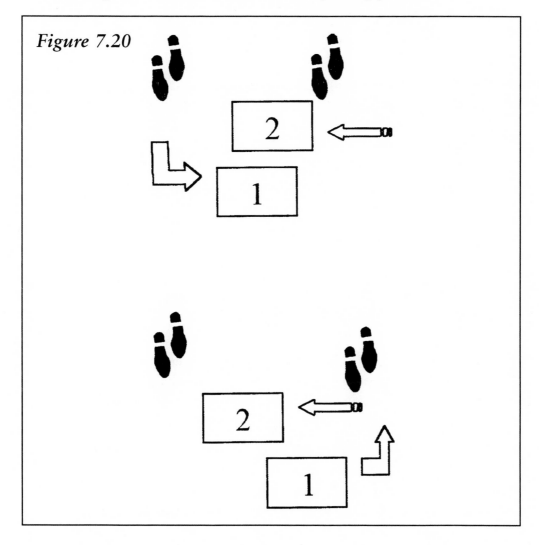

Figure 7.20

JUST FOR FUN: A MISCELLANY
OF MARVELOUS MOVES

Follow the Leader

The name says it all. In this routine, the line of carts simply follows the leader all through the street. It can be done with either a single or double vertical line. Usually the line swerves across the width of the street from curb to curb, forming a continuous "s," but anything is possible. If the parade stops, the leader can even bring the carts around into a full circle.

Green Eggs and Ham

You can do it on the street
Do it to a crazy beat

You can do it in your sleep
You can do a jump or leap

You can do it in the sun
Anyway it's lots of fun

Whether you're a Sal or Sam
You will like Green Eggs and Ham

Green Eggs and Ham is easy and fun. When the signal is given, everyone scrambles off in every direction, goes wild and has a great time. Then at the next signal, everyone politely returns to the original formation.

The drill team at the Santa Cruz Public Library has added several twists to this simple routine that make it even more fun, especially for the audience. They start with the "Follow the Leader" routine. When their leader yells, "Circulate," everyone scurries off every which way whooping and hollering. They stay relatively close, within a six-foot radius or so. Then the leader approaches the group, puts her finger to her lips and says, "Shush!" Others then take up the "Shushing" and march back into the original lines. They try to look very serious. Like all "Shushing" routines, it is a crowd favorite.

Skating

One of the Lincoln Public Library Cartwheelers' favorite moves is the Skate. It's simple to do. Push the cart, put a foot on the lower shelf and extend the other leg. Momentum carries the cart forward. Be sure there are no potholes or rocks in the way. This could be fun if the group is going downhill, as long as it's not too steep. Also, be sure the carts can take the weight of the person skating. This is probably best performed by the smaller members of the team.

Dancing

If you feel it's time to kick up your heels, a book cart can be a great partner, just be prepared to lead.

Wiggles

When just plain marching doesn't seem frisky enough, try pushing the back of the cart side to side. This will create a kind of wiggle movement that will liven up the action. To take it a step further, team members can sway their hips in the opposite direction. Ready? Rumba.

Kicks

It may not be Route 66, but you can still get in some kicks. (If you got this old reference, it doesn't mean that you are too old to be in the parade. We wrote it and we're still in there kicking.) There are a wide variety of kick steps that can be performed with a book cart. It works great since carts provide support and balance when needed. Just be sure not to kick the cart. It really hurts.

Small kicks to the side are the easiest. When kicking across the other leg, be sure to swing the cart in the opposite direction to create enough room. Adding a can-can type knee plus kick action can be very impressive, but tiring. For the truly fit, try kicking heels together while holding onto the cart for support.

Clogging

Instead of merely walking behind a cart, the fancy footed may prefer to clog, tap or skip along the street. This can be an individual activity or the whole group can form their own dance company. A long parade of clogging or tapping would require very strong ankles. It may be best to reserve these fancy steps for selected times or short parades. But if being in a parade makes you feel like dancing, go for it.

· 8 ·

Before the Parade Passes By: Stationary Routines

Sooner or later the forward progress of the parade will stop. In the larger parades, especially those with television coverage, there is usually a grandstand area where groups can pause and show off. Sometimes this location also hosts the judges for the parade.

At other times, technical difficulties can put a halt to the parade. In small-town parades with a casual atmosphere, the forward movement can just stop whenever someone wants it to. For all of these scenarios, the smart book cart drill team will have at least one snappy move to entertain the crowd. This chapter offers some possibilities.

The main thing is to keep in motion to give the crowd something to look at. One very good way to do this is to move in circles. Big or small circles are the basic formation for several fancy maneuvers, as well as just looking good on their own. Simply forming a basic circle will likely bring on a round of applause, and the circle can be embellished to surprise and further please the crowd.

If your marchers are tired of circling, let the carts do the work. Book cart wheels can go in any direction, which makes them great for spinning. There are lots of ways to make carts go round and round—just be sure your marchers don't get dizzy!

This chapter offers variations on both the basic circle and the basic spin. At the end are a few fun maneuvers using books as props. Use any or all of these ideas to keep things moving when the rest of the parade stands still.

CIRCLE VARIATION NO. 1: CAROUSEL

An easy way to form a circle is to have the lead cart swerve toward one side with everyone following in line. Eventually, the lead cart begins to curve back around until the circle is formed. If starting from a double line, each pair should fall into single file as the circle is formed. Finally, the leader will pull up behind the last cart in line, closing the circle.

Once the circle is formed, the group can reverse direction by turning their carts 180 degrees and heading in the opposite direction. Or the group can stop, with only the people turning around to grab the cart that was behind them, and start off in this new direction.

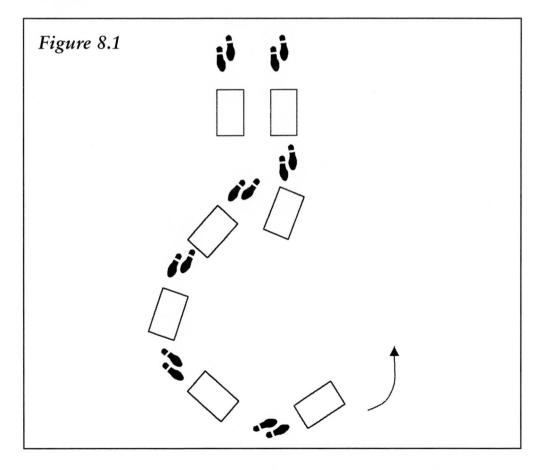

Figure 8.1

CIRCLE VARIATION NO. 2:
DOUBLE CIRCLES

If starting from a double line formation, there are several options for forming circles. The lines can stay together and form a double circle, with one line on the outside and the other on the inside.

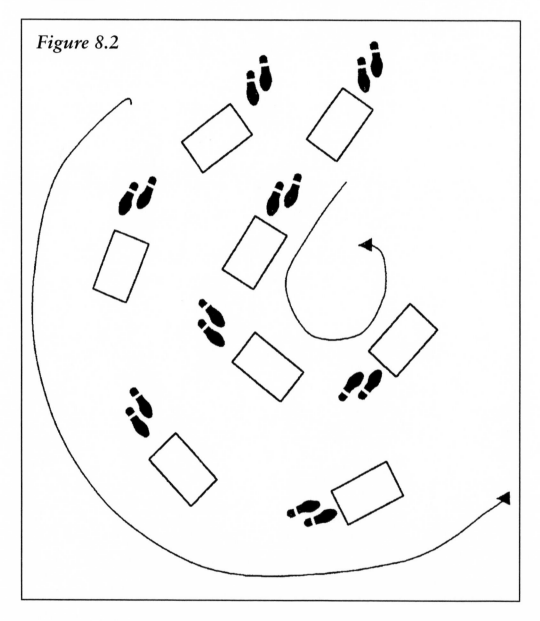

Figure 8.2

The outside line will be spaced much further apart and will need to maintain a faster pace than the inside line. A double circle is particularly impressive if at some point the inside and outside lines go in opposite directions.

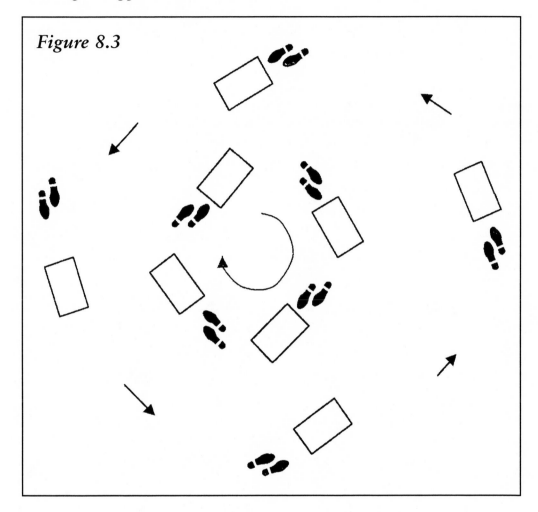

Figure 8.3

CIRCLE VARIATION NO. 3: CIRCLE THE WAGONS

The Fairfax City Regional Library performs a circle variation that they call "Circle the Wagons." According to Suzanne Levy, they start with four lines. The leaders of the two middle lines move forward and turn to their respective curbs. They circle around to surround the middle two rows, who march in place.

If beginning with only two lines, the group could have the last cart in each line remain in place while the rest of the line circles around it. Be sure to have the lines spaced wide apart before beginning, so there will be enough room to form the circles.

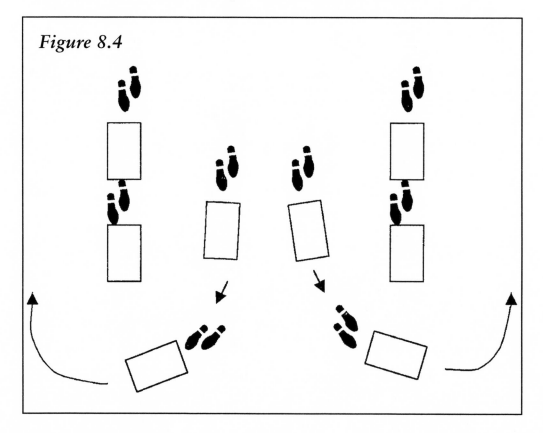

Figure 8.4

CIRCLE VARIATION NO. 4: PINWHEEL

Those great June Taylor dancers from the old Jackie Gleason show inspired the Pinwheel formation. You have to envision the maneuver from the sky to get that pinwheel vision. Once the carts are brought together to form the pinwheel, there are an endless variety of showy moves that can be made. A real crowd favorite is the "Shushing" move shown first. This routine does take a few minutes to perform and can only be performed while the parade is stopped. But it is worth holding up the parade, since it is a real showstopper. It also works great for indoor shows.

From our experience, this move works best with four carts in each pinwheel, but other numbers are possible. Here are the four steps for this impressive maneuver.

1. Form small circles. From two straight lines, veer toward the outside, following the front carts around to form two small circles. If there is only one line, go in either direction. If there are eight or more carts per line, each fifth cart in each line begins a new circle. Or if only four more carts follow, they would form one circle, as pictured in Figure 8.5 (next page).

The leader should be careful to watch the formation of the circles. Make sure all circles are formed before proceeding to the next step.

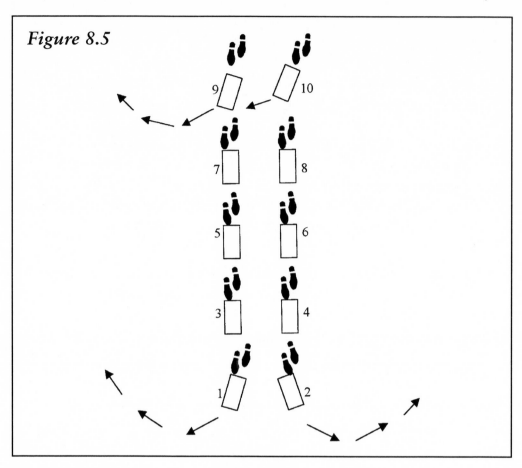

Figure 8.5

Figure 8.6

The next drawing illustrates the continuing formation of the circles.

Figure 8.7

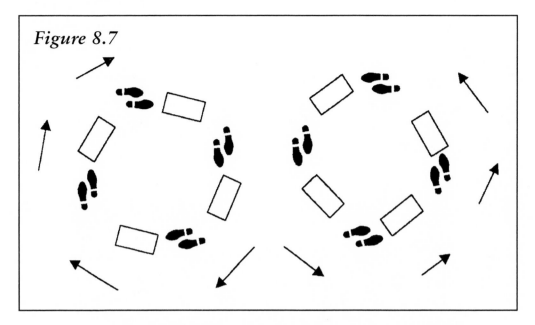

2. Form the pinwheel by turning the carts in toward the center of the circle so that the ends meet and form a square. Next comes the tricky part.

Clockwise carts: When the carts meet, change the holds on the cart so that right hands hold the handles of both the cart in front and behind each person. The left hand holds the handle on the outside of the circle. The cart is now being pushed in a sideways position.

Counter-clockwise carts: Left hands will be holding the carts in the center, and right hands on the outside.

Keep moving around in a circle while forming the pinwheel. (Note: Holding on to the carts is much easier if all the carts in the circle are the same heights.) Continue to march in the same direction. Again, the leader needs to be sure that all the pinwheels have been formed before proceeding to the next step.

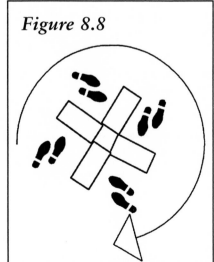

Figure 8.8

The Pierce County Library drill team forms a perfect pinwheel (photograph by Lynne Zeiher).

Step 3. Shhing: When everyone has a firm grip on the carts, and the circle is moving well, it's time for the fun part—the "Shushing." At the leader's signal, each person lets go of the cart, turns toward the outside, and, while "Shushing," rotates until facing the cart behind them. Using a count of eight seems to work well.

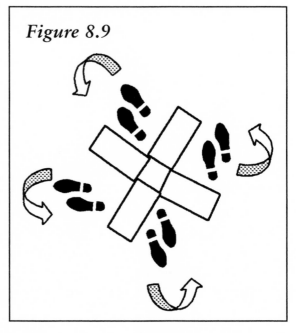

Figure 8.9

Shushing the crowd in Gig Harbor, Washington (photograph by Judith Prowse Buskirk).

With everyone facing the opposite direction, grab the cart handles again and move the entire circle as before. This time, everyone will be going in the opposite direction.

The crowd will be impressed by the formation of the pinwheel and be cheering your fabulous move. The "shushing" move usually quiets the crowd. Then they laugh uncontrollably (well, at least out loud). Repeating the shushing move works well.

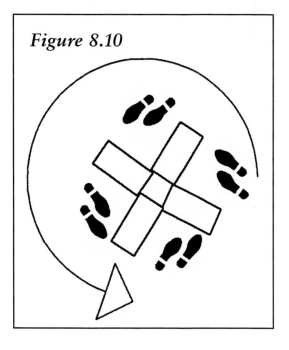

Figure 8.10

4. Back in line. After the crowd has been thoroughly
   impressed, it's time to move back into the basic line formation. Continue to move around in the pinwheel circle until
   the leader signals time to move out. The person in each circle who started that circle breaks out of the pinwheel, grabs
   the end of their cart and heads back in the direction of the
   parade flow. All the carts in that circle follow back into the
   original parade formation.

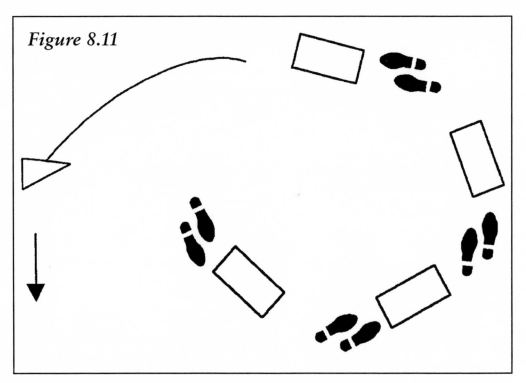

Figure 8.11

CIRCLE VARIATION NO. 5: SPOKE

This is an impressive move, but not hard to do. It takes a bit of time to set up, especially if the group is large. Basically, the group moves in a straight line around in a big circle, as if they were the spokes of a big wheel.

The Spoke maneuver can be done with as few as four carts and as many as the street or area will hold. It starts with all the carts lined up perpendicular to the curb. (See "Fan Out" maneuver for ways to achieve this formation.)

1. From Fan Out formation, either the even or odd numbered carts reverses their direction. It is easiest to have each person turn around, one at a time, starting on the outside of the line.

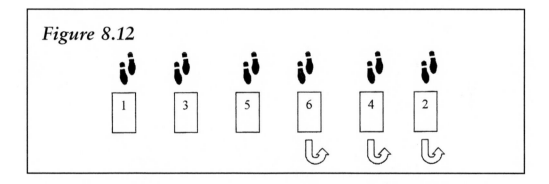

Figure 8.12

This formation can also be done with the carts in the sideways position. This works especially well if you have a small group.

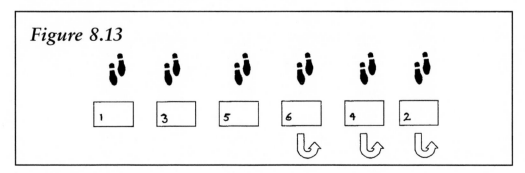

Figure 8.13

2. Move carts as close to center as possible. It is helpful to butt the carts together and try to hold the handles of two side-by-side carts together.

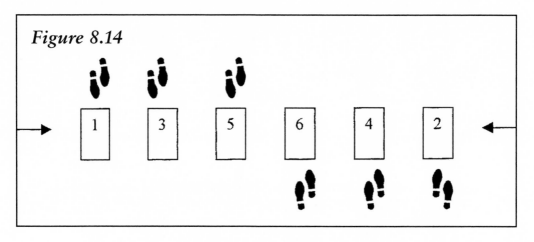

Figure 8.14

All carts move forward like the spoke in a wheel. The center carts need to take very small steps, while those on the outside move more quickly. Make at least one full rotation. Try to keep the line as straight as possible.

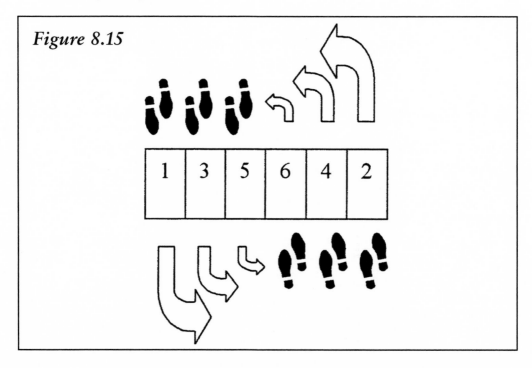

Figure 8.15

The Pierce County Library team marches around and around doing the Spoke routine (photograph by Judith Prowse Buskirk).

3. After completing one or more rotations, the even numbered carts repeat the reverse move so that they are once again

Figure 8.16

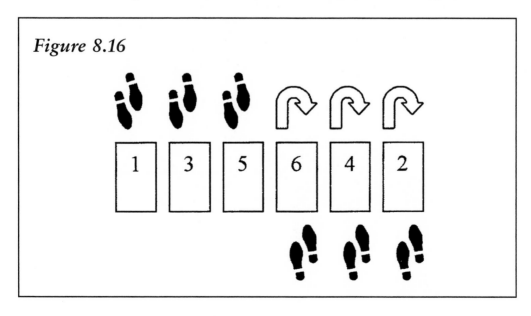

facing forward. The group can then march forward in the horizontal line or use the "Fan In" maneuver to return to the standard double line formation.

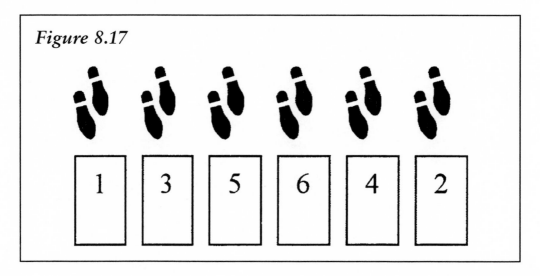

Figure 8.17

SPINNING VARIATION NO. 1:
SPIN CYCLE

Whenever the parade gets a bit boring, throw in a wild spin cycle. The leader gives the signal, then everyone spins their cart around and around. Everyone spins at his or her own speed and direction. Showoffs may even do one-handed spins.

This maneuver can be done while marching forward or from a stopped position, and for as long as needed. But be sure not to go too long, or the group may have trouble walking a straight line for the rest of the parade.

Figure 8.18

Joanie Wood (center) of the Pierce County Library really gets into putting the perfect spin on her cart (photograph by Lynne Zeiher).

SPINNING VARIATION NO. 2:
PRECISION TURN

For a more controlled look, decide on which direction to go, clockwise or counterclockwise. Use a signal to start a full or half spin. A fun variation is to have each pair spin one after the other down the line, i.e. 1 & 2 spin once, then 3 & 4, then 5 & 6 and so on to the end of the line. Then 1 & 2 start the process again.

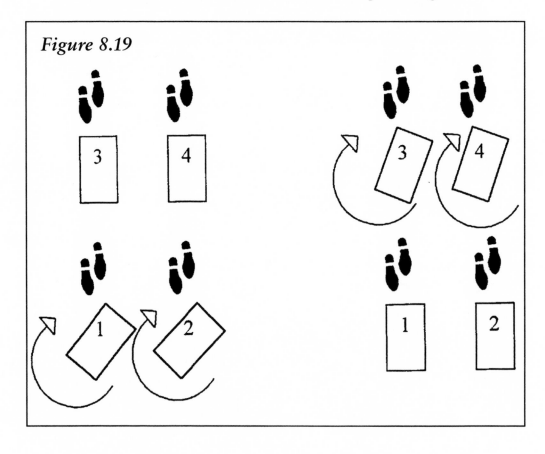

Figure 8.19

SPINNING VARIATION NO. 3: ROMANTIC TWIRL

This was inspired by an indoor routine done to the song "Marion the Librarian" from *The Music Man*. During the bridge section of the song the tempo changes from a march beat to a more swaying style. At a rehearsal Pierce County team members got really silly and started swirling the carts around. The romantic twirl was invented. Think about those romantic movies (or even commercials) where a couple hold hands and twirl around in an open field of wildflowers and you've captured the essence of the romantic twirl. Hold the end of the cart with both arms locked straight. Spin around in place while the cart moves around in a big circle

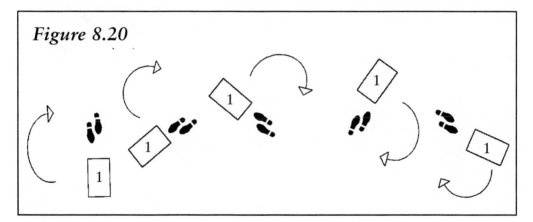

Figure 8.20

Be sure there is plenty of room for each person and that all the wheels are securely attached to the cart. If the cart is spun fast enough it has a tendency to rear up into a wheelie. A loose wheel could fly off and cause serious injury.

SPINNING VARIATION NO. 4:
WALKABOUT

In this spin the cart stays in place, pivots from the center, and the person walks around it. Hold the cart at the end, twist so the body is perpendicular to the cart, and go.

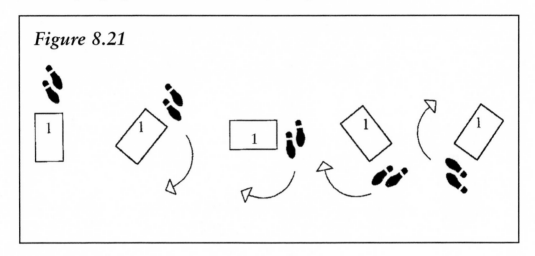

Figure 8.21

BOOK HANDLING

If the group has brought along books or other props, there are lots of fun things to do with them. Just be sure that the props are securely fastened to the carts, or everyone will lose them long before the trick begins. The props will also need to be easily retrievable and restored. Bungee cords have worked well for some groups. Attaching some type of pocket on the inside of the cart may also provide a workable solution.

Circulate: Book Passing—Form a circle using the previous instructions. Once the circle is formed, stop and turn the front of the carts toward the center.

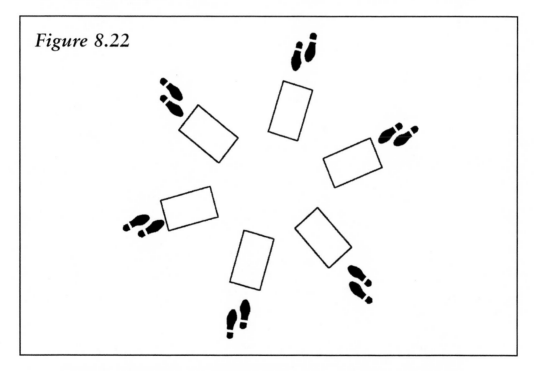

Figure 8.22

At the signal (the Alaska Library Association group uses the signal "circulate"), each team member takes his/her book and passes it to the person to their right. Keep passing for a designated number of times or until signaled to stop or to reverse. It may take a little practice to get a passing rhythm that has that precision look.

(Hint: Large circles may need to close the gap between the carts by moving in toward the center so the space between each cart is within passing distance.)

Check Them Out: Tossing—If the circle is small enough, consider tossing the books to the carter directly across the circle. Everyone needs to take turns hurling his/her book to the person on the opposite side of the circle. Have only one book flying across at a time or risk mid-air collisions. Designate who will start and the order in which the action will proceed. It is helpful to count off each toss so everyone knows whose turn it is.

Take a Break: Reading—This can also be a good time to pretend to read the books, dance them around or just take a break. Of course, this can be done at anytime, not just when the team is in a circle formation.

If the parade becomes too strenuous, take a break and read, like the Cart Wheelers of Lincoln County Library (photograph by Julie Wullner).

· 9 ·

Backup Plan:
Reverse Moves for Routines

A reverse move is a simple maneuver that can be done as a stationary move or while the parade is advancing. The group may fall behind a bit as the parade moves forward, but not too far. It also works great for momentary lulls, since it doesn't take long to complete one rotation. Variations can be very fun and impressive.

The Pierce County Library completes another successful Reverse routine (photograph by Lynne Zeiher).

BASIC REVERSE

Start with two vertical lines. At the signal, the two front carts turn to the outside and head toward the back of the line.

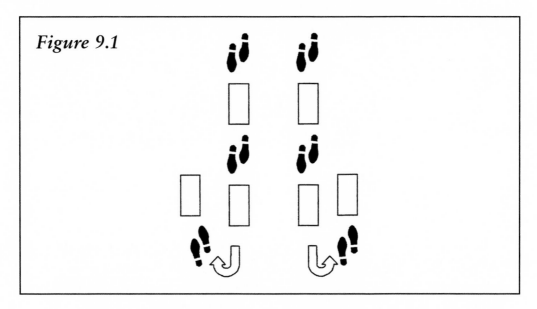

Figure 9.1

When the first pair returns to the front, the maneuver can be repeated, or not. It is helpful for the leader to stand at the position where each cart turns to begin the reverse move.

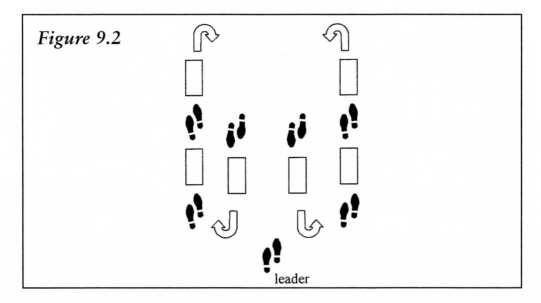

Figure 9.2

leader

BIG DEWEY

The Book Cart Drill Team from the Santa Cruz Public Library in California performs a variation of the Reverse that is appropriately called the Big Dewey. Instead of staying close to the original line, the turning carts veer out, forming a large D.

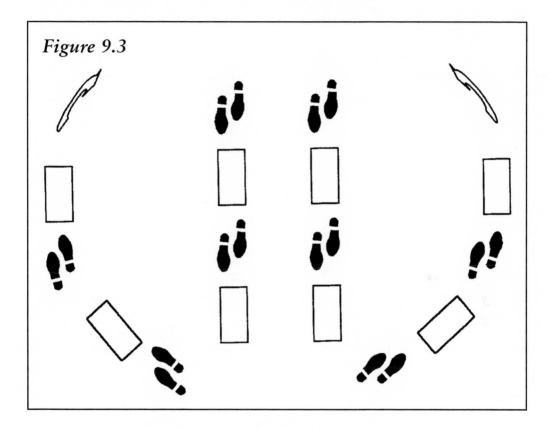

Figure 9.3

MOVING PASSES

The drill team from the Eldersburg Branch of the Carroll County Public Library puts a reverse twist on the reverse. No one actually heads in the opposite direction, but the front pair stays put and allows the other members to pass them. Each pair in turn falls to the back until the original front pair is returned to their beginning position.

1. Start from a double line formation where the lines are spaced well apart from each other. The front pair moves toward the center.

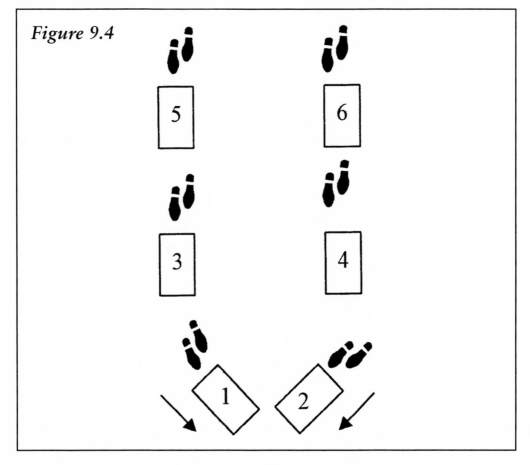

Figure 9.4

2. While carters one and two march in place, the lines proceed past them (see Figure 9.5).

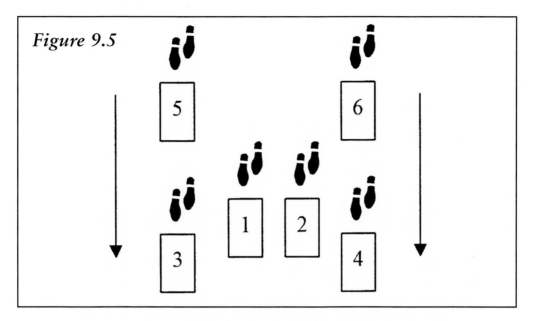

Figure 9.5

3. Once the line has passed the stationary carts, they angle back into line, and the pair now in front move toward the center.

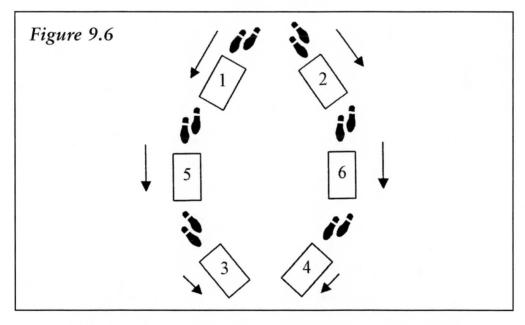

Figure 9.6

4. Once the new front pair has moved to the center, the others pass by them as before. These steps continue until the first pair is back in front.

OTHER REVERSE VARIATIONS

High Five

In another version of the Basic Reverse, instead of veering wide apart as in the Big Dewey, the reversing carts stay close to the original line. As each person passes, teammates give each other a high five. It can get tricky at the beginning and end of the line, so be sure the group doesn't sacrifice cart control when making contact.

Solo Spotlight

The Lincoln Library Cart Wheelers' version of the Reverse allows for some self-expression and personal attention. As each pair reaches the front of the line, they have the option of performing a variety of fancy moves—acrobatic split jumps, heel clicks or just simple waves to the crowd. The possibilities are limited only by the team members' imagination and physical abilities.

A Lincoln Library Cart Wheeler shows off at the front of the line (photograph by Julie Wullner).

· 10 ·

Curtain Up: Stage Routines

For those special occasions when the group does a stage performance, it works best to have a set of movements choreographed for a smooth transition from one move to the next. During a parade most of the action is concentrated on forward movements, with an occasional stop to perform a special routine (such as the pinwheel or spoke).

Since the audience changes constantly as the group moves along, there is time to switch from one routine to another at random with periods of time when the group just marches forward and waves. In a stage performance the crowd will be continually entertained if there is a well-choreographed routine.

Musical accompaniment can play an intricate part in these presentations. Routines have been choreographed using a wide variety of musical choices, from the upbeat contemporary "Nine to Five" to the traditional show tune " Marion the Librarian" from *The Music Man* and the "Library Card Song" from the *Arthur* television show.

Music is not required, but it can add that special flair that makes the performance sparkle. It also can help keep the group synchronized as they groove to the beat.

ESTHER WILLIAMS ROUTINE

This routine was choreographed by Kathleen Kelly MacMillan from the Carr County Public Library's branch in Eldersburg, Maryland. Since it is performed in 3/4 time, she suggests playing a waltz if music is added. The numbers in the instructions refer to the number of 3-counts for each move. Kathleen named the routine after Esther Williams since it was her synchronized swimming moves that inspired it. We would strongly suggest that it not be performed in a swimming pool, however, since metal carts don't work well in water.

1. Begin in a basic double vertical line.
    Turn out 1
    Move out 2
    Turn forward 1

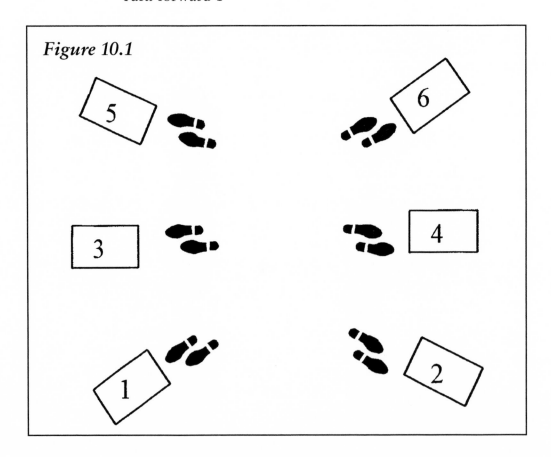

Figure 10.1

2. Inward Reverse 1 and 2.

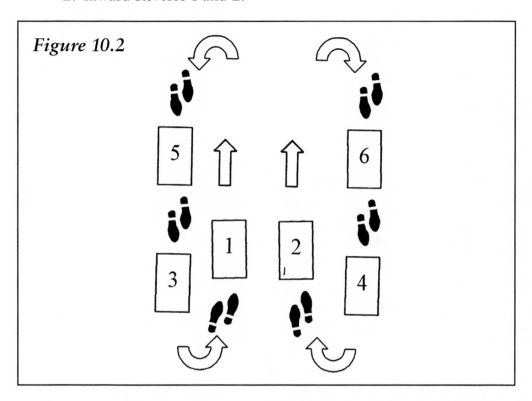

Figure 10.2

3. All carts spin once then move forward one. Repeat four times.

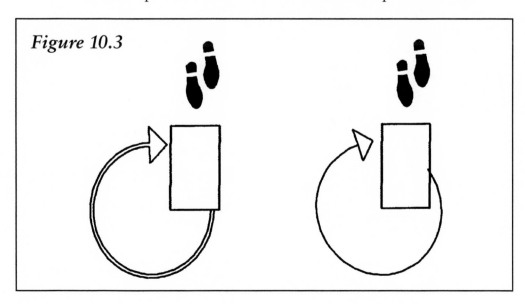

Figure 10.3

4. a) Turn in 1
   b) Turn out 1
   c) Push cart out 1
   d) Push cart in 1 (Do Push/Pull movie twice)

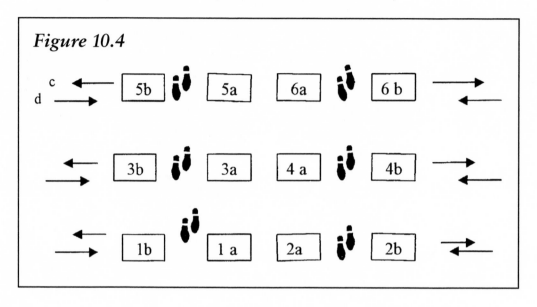

Figure 10.4

5. Turn forward 1
   Turn in 1
   Move in 1
   Hold 1

   Staggered Wave left 2
   Staggered Wave right 2 (Wave left/right twice)
   Hold one

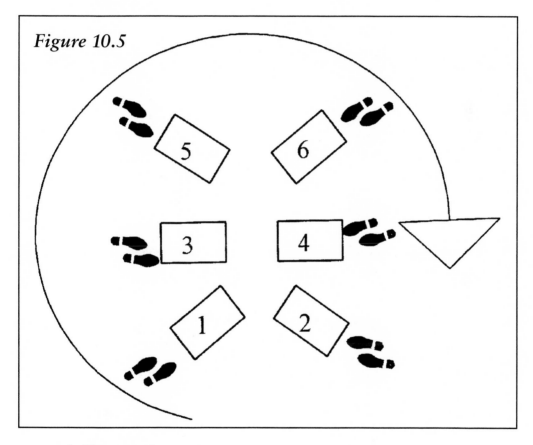

Figure 10.5

6. Turn out 1
   Push cart out 1
   Pull cart in 1 (Do push/pull move twice)
   Hold 1

   Staggered Wave right 2
   Staggered Wave left 2 (Wave right/left twice)
   Hold 1

7. Spin carts 1
   Turn carts to form circle 1
   Hold 1

   Face out, circle clockwise 8 (Bodies face out and reach back
      to hold on to both ends of the cart.)
   Face out, circle counter clockwise 8

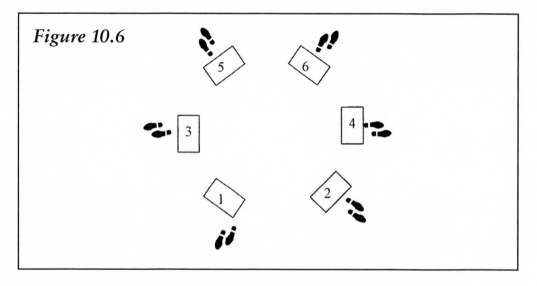

Figure 10.6

8. Move back to end of cart facing clockwise 1
   Hold cart 1
   Unspiral circle with cart 1 leading

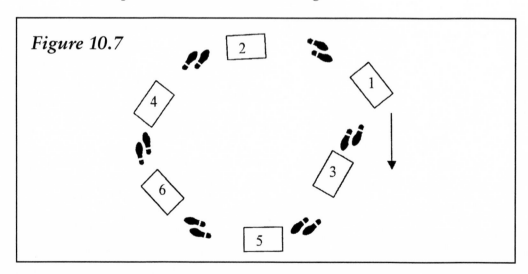

Figure 10.7

9. Hold 1
    Turn out carts (Staggered) 1
    a) Push cart out 1
        Pull cart in then turn 1
    b) Push cart out 1
        Pull cart in, then turn 1 (Do a and b twice)

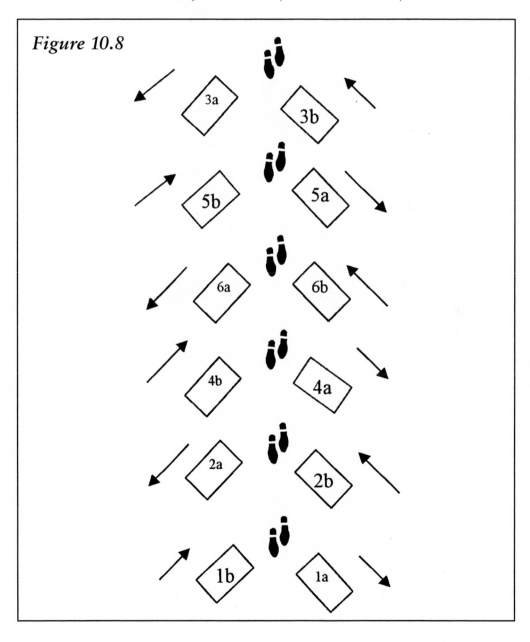

Figure 10.8

10. Form circle moving clockwise

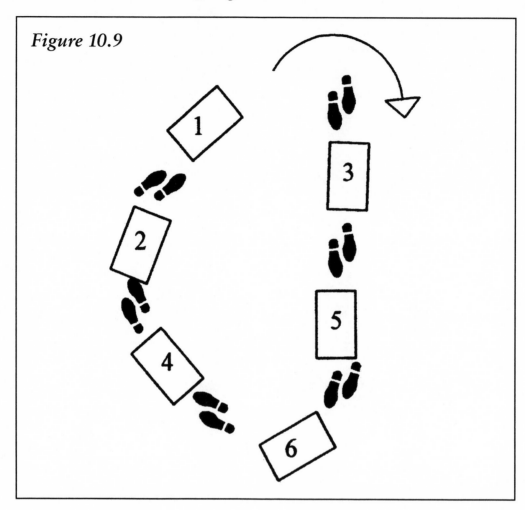

Figure 10.9

11. Move in circle. Each cart then stops in its original position. (Note: Carts 3 and 5 will pass by 1 to return to their original spots.)
    Spin 1

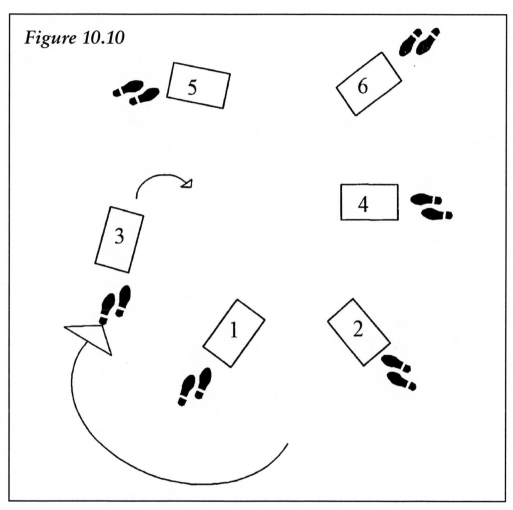

Figure 10.10

12. Turn to face forward
    Perform criss cross routine (as many as space allows)

13. Return to original positions
    Spin 1 (two times)
    Move out 1
    Spin 1 (three times for big finish)

· 11 ·

Tricks of the Trade: What We Wish We'd Known

Lessons learned through experience seem to be the most painful. In this book we want to share some things we've learned the hard way. That doesn't mean we know everything—but we can pass on some tips that may make your experience more fun.

Those Tricky Carts

Anyone who has worked in a library knows that book carts often develop an independent spirit: They simply will not do what they're pushed to do. That can spell trouble for a book cart drill team. There are some things that can be done to get them to behave on parade day.

Care and Feeding of Cart Wheels

The only moving parts on a book cart are the wheels. That's where you need to focus attention. Wheels will work smoothly when treated to a little tender care. WD40 can be your cart's best friend: A spray of lubricant can loosen the most stubborn wheel, greatly improving the cart's maneuverability. Ask your maintenance department for help; this is a way for them to be involved in the drill team, too.

Besides wheels that grab, watch out for wheels that fall off easily. Loose wheels find the worst times to fall off—when crossing railroad tracks or dodging potholes. Before each performance, check those wheels. Repair or replace them as needed. It's a good idea to take a few tools to performances—just in case there's trouble on parade day.

Transportation Issues

Getting book cart drill team members to a performance is pretty easy. The book carts can be an entirely different matter. The carts won't roll there on their own.

Is There a Van or Truck Big Enough?

Most libraries probably have a bookmobile or delivery van large enough to haul the book carts. That's the ideal situation. If the library vehicle isn't large enough to hold all of the carts, it may be necessary to make more than one trip to the start of the parade. Ask the library's driver to help out with transportation. This would be a good way to give another staff member the chance to be part of the team.

You might find a staff member who has a private vehicle that would be ideal for this job. Here's another chance to involve more people in the drill team. Make sure that there is proper insurance for whoever drives the vehicle to the drill team's performances.

If the library does not have a suitable vehicle, and you can't find one from a staff member, you will need to secure outside help. Ask around your community. This would be a good opportunity for a local business to participate by lending a truck and driver. Be sure to give them credit as a contributor in all of your publicity.

Who Will Drive?

If the library vehicle is being used to transport the book carts, why not ask the person most familiar with that vehicle to drive it?

Ask your bookmobile driver or delivery person. They already know the vehicle; and, chances are, they are familiar with the streets in your town. You know that they are good at their job and that the team can depend on them.

If you have borrowed a private vehicle, ask the owner to drive it. Include them in the planning and give them credit for their donation.

A local business that donates their vehicle might be willing to recruit a driver from among their employees. Make sure that you acknowledge their contribution and express your appreciation—in writing and publicly, if possible.

Check with your business office about insurance on whatever vehicle you will be using. Who is responsible for insurance? Is there any extra cost involved? Who will pay? Make sure that whoever drives the library's vehicle is authorized to do so.

Where to Unload and Reload

If you're using a bookmobile or large commercial truck to haul the book carts, a little scouting trip would make parade day much easier. Parades bring together lots of people and vehicles. That spells congestion. Maneuvering a big rig will be tricky, and finding a good spot to unload could be very hard. Good planning is a must.

After entering the parade, you will be sent instructions for the big day. You may even be given your number in the line-up. Parade officials will send information about the assembling area, what the parade route will be, and where the parade will end. This is all very important information for the transportation folks.

Unless they are very familiar with the town, they may want to have a practice of their own. They'll need to find the best route to the assembling area, taking into account the size of the vehicle and the congestion on parade day. This is the time to find a good spot to unload the carts and the drill team.

Then it's off to the pick-up point, remembering to avoid the parade route. Once there, they will need to find a spot to reload the book carts and pick up the drill team.

This part of the planning is much easier if the bookmobile or van is part of your parade unit. No need to do all the planning—you'll have your ride with you.

Get Ready to Rumble

Book carts are usually very quiet, smooth-running contraptions; we push them around our libraries every day. But get them out of the library into the streets and you'll be amazed. Those small, hard rubber wheels will be rolling over the same pavement that usually sees only large, inflated tires. That rumble you hear and feel as you drive your car down the street will be magnified many, many times when you are pushing a book cart.

If you plan to carry anything on the book carts, strap it down. If you don't, it will end up bouncing right off the cart. The cart decorators will need to keep this in mind when planning their beautification project. Drill team members will be using both hands to guide the carts and will not be able to hold decorations on too! Glue, tie, tape or strap everything in place.

Gloves are comfortable, if it's not over 80°. The vibrations from the cart wheels will feel very like a massage for your hands and arms. Some nice, soft cotton gloves will help to cushion your hands from the vibrations and from the hard edges of the book carts. The inexpensive garden glove works well, and can be a colorful part of your uniform. After one parade, you'll be glad you wore the gloves. In cooler weather those colorful "magic" gloves that stretch to any size are an inexpensive option for the team. The colors can be part of the group's fashion statement.

Road Hazards

Bumpy streets are not the only road hazards you may face during a parade. From a car, you are not bothered by some things that can cause trouble for book carts.

Potholes and Railroad Tracks

Two of the major obstacles for book cart drill teams are potholes and railroad tracks; they're annoying in a car but frightening for a book cart drill team. If a wheel drops into a pothole or a drill team member steps in one, disaster may ensue, with book cart and hapless marcher struggling to regain solid footing. A twisted ankle or an overturned book cart could spell disaster for the team.

Besides being noisy, annoying bumps in the street, railroad tracks hold hidden dangers. There are deep grooves on either side of the tracks. Unless the book cart wheels meet the railroad track at a perpendicular angle, a wheel could drop into that groove, upsetting book cart and drill team member.

Don't Lose Your Wheels

This is when all of that time spent caring for those book cart wheels will pay off. If the wheels are securely fastened and in good working order, even if one should encounter a railroad track or pothole, the wheel should at least stay attached to the book cart. If one of the wheels is loose, you can bet this is the time that it will fall off—the least convenient time possible. This is a minor disaster that can easily be prevented by good maintenance of the book carts, and by attention paid to road hazards.

Beware Equestrian Units

Railroad tracks and potholes are not all that you need to watch out for along the parade route. In many communities, equestrian units are part of every parade. Hopefully, the library's book cart drill team will not get stuck directly behind one.

Horses will invariably take care of bodily functions at the most inopportune times. For unprepared drill teams this can be a very unpleasant, smelly, and slippery experience. Hopefully, there will be enough flexibility in your routines to allow sudden sidesteps or other avoidance maneuvers. Avoiding animal deposits should take precedence over precision every time. The maneuver will be over quickly, but a wheel that runs through an unpleasant pile will be with the group for the entire parade. If an accident like this does occur, be sure that the wheels and shoes get cleaned up before heading back to the library.

"What Did You Say?" The Noise Factor

When the book carts hit the road, the first thing that you will notice is the rumbling and vibrating of those trusty steeds. We push book carts over quiet carpeted floors, never knowing that anything that runs so silently could possibly make such a terrible racket when turned loose on public streets.

They are so noisy that it is imperative to develop a means of communicating with the team beyond just shouting. For an inside performance, a microphone may be all that is needed. If the library has access to a bullhorn or other portable voice-amplifying device, it can be possible to talk the group through their paces during a parade as well. However, most groups will need to be a bit more creative.

A simple whistle and a series of signals can serve as an effective alternative to a bullhorn. In our case, one whistle blow alerts the carters to watch for the beginning of a new routine. Two toots signal the start of the maneuver, and three the end.

Communicating which routine to do next can be accomplished by several means as well. We use laminated cardboard cards with the names of the routines in big bold letters to announce the next move. For convenience, the cards are held together by big metal rings. The leader flips through the routines, signals for attention, and holds the card high so everyone can see it.

Another alternative would be to have each routine numbered and hold up the proper number of fingers to signal the next routine. If using this method, it is advisable to have a cheat sheet with the numbering system taped on each cart to avoid confusion.

A simple sign with large lettering lets the team know what to do next (photograph by Judith Prowse Buskirk).

Weather: Be Prepared

If the book cart drill team is performing out of doors, weather is an important factor to consider.

Don't Rain on My Parade

Most towns hold their community parades during the summer months. The weather is generally cooperative during that time of year. But some have celebrations at other times of the year, i.e., Easter, Christmas and Veterans' Day. These are times that the weather may be a big factor.

For those of us who live in the soggy parts of the country, rain on parade day is always a possibility. If you are in enough parades, eventually it will rain on the drill team. Don't let it ruin your fun. Brightly colored ponchos can be part of the drill team's uniform; you can usually find inexpensive, bright yellow ones at sporting goods stores.

Take into account the possibility of rain when planning the cart decorations. Laminate paper signs; use plastic flowers, streamers, etc.; or use natural materials that don't mind getting a little wet. In Yakima we even made a clear plastic cover for our banner, which was made of felt. You can imagine how heavy that would get when wet. Take a little time to plan for that rain, and it won't spoil your big day.

Pushing a Cart Can Work Up a Sweat

In some parts of the country heat can be just as annoying as rain. Imagine how hot a metal book cart can get when the sun is beating down on the parade and the air temperature is over 80 degrees. Pushing a book cart through intricate routines can be very draining. Those gloves that are worn to protect from vibrations will also help in the heat. Cotton gloves help to absorb perspiration, keeping hands dry. In heat, hats help to give you a cool head. And keeping a supply of water on hand will help team members keep cool and have fun during the parade.

BRRRRRRR

Those versatile hats and gloves will also help when parade day falls on one of the coldest days of the summer. If your town's celebration is in any season other than summer, wearing warm hats and gloves will be a necessity. Keeping those head and hands warm will make a big difference in how energetic the drill team feels, how well they perform and how much fun they have. You might even plan for a hot beverage at the end of the parade route for the hearty souls who braved the cold.

Medical Emergencies

By their very nature emergencies are hard to plan for; but not being prepared for the unexpected can spell disaster for the drill team. For the Yakima drill team, the largest parade of the year took its toll on one of our team members. The weather was very warm. The parade contained mostly mechanized vehicles and moved very fast. The unit we followed moved back and forth along the parade route (a big no-no) and left big gaps in the parade. The parade officials tried to force us to speed up in order to close the gaps.

All of these factors contributed to our emergency. One of our team members became overheated, nearly passing out at the wheel. She did have the good sense to drop out of the parade; it's a good thing that it was near an ambulance crew and their vehicle. She didn't need their help, but we felt better about leaving her with them close by.

We learned a very big lesson that day. We had not planned on how to help one of our team members in case of an emergency. And we had not planned on how to continue our routines with someone missing. That's a mistake that we won't repeat.

Having a library vehicle as part of your unit will ensure that there is a way to remove a team member should they need medical treatment. The driver should be someone that has been trained in first aid, if possible. If you don't have a vehicle, plan for one of the marchers to drop out to lend assistance. Or have staff members who are not participating in the parade placed along the route. In case of an emergency, they can help.

That will take care of the most important part of the emergency. Then, as you plan the routines for your parade, imagine how you would continue if one of the drill team members had to drop out of the parade. Knowing that it can happen, and planning what to do, helps take some of the anxiety out of the emergency.

· 12 ·

Tell the World:
Publicity for Your Team

When the best ever precision book cart drill team is ready to perform, tell everyone. Here's your chance to show the world what lots of hard work and good planning can produce. Don't be afraid to toot your horn. If you have a public relations department, work with them to spread the word. If not, forge ahead on your own.

At the next general staff meeting, show off the drill team. At a Pierce County staff meeting, the team performed in the parking lot in front of the building. Staff members looked on from the sidewalks and from the windows on the second floor. It was a great break from the business of the day, yet was still work related. Use other staff functions as a way to publicize the drill team. This gives everyone a chance to help celebrate something they may have helped to produce. You may also acquire some new recruits.

Write an article for your staff newsletter. Include a photo if you can. Don't forget to mention all of your awards. And thank all of those who helped make the drill team a success. Each time that the drill team appears in a parade, send in a few tidbits for the newsletter. Include stories of special incidents that have occurred, such as patrons who recognized you or a renegade wheel that went astray. If nothing else, list the team members that participated in that parade. They deserve credit each time they perform. The drill team story could also be told in your Friends' newsletter. If your library produces a newsletter for the community, the drill team would make a great front-page story.

But don't stop there. Local newspapers will probably cover the parades you participate in. Don't hesitate to help them out by submitting a description of your drill team. Contact a reporter you might know and offer them additional information about the drill team. They will probably want to know how the team got started, why the library does this, etc. Be ready with some interesting human-interest stories from your experiences. Who knows, they may even decide to do a feature story, complete with photographs. If the team has appeared in parades in previous years but not been featured in the paper, contact the paper a month before the next appearance so they will have the option of covering the drill team either before or after the event.

Local television may jump at the chance to feature the drill team. How many times have they visited the library for some event and gone away disappointed because library business isn't action packed. Here's your chance to change that. Imagine, a "snapshot" of the library that moves! Television stations want stories with interesting moving pictures for news and local talk shows. Offer to give them a live demonstration or give them a video of your best performance if you have one worth televising. Make a personal visit and take along a picture to show them just what a treat they will have on parade day.

Why stop with the local media? Tell the rest of the universe about your library's drill team. Almost every regional and national professional library association has their own publication. Write to all of them, enclosing a photo of your drill team in action. This may be just the story they need to add some zip to their next issue.

Take advantage of the Internet. Everybody's surfing the Net these days. Use that to your advantage. You probably belong to at least one listserv. Use that as another way to tell people about your drill team. Your library probably has a web page. Spread the good news about the book cart drill team throughout cyberspace, or at least your own corner of it. Check with the people that manage the web page about including the drill team. Several libraries, such as Bettendorf Public Library in Iowa, have group photos as well as action shots on the Net. Wouldn't a short video be a great addition? It would really bring the library's web site to life.

If your library doesn't have a web page, contact your state library or your state's library association. They may be glad to include your library's drill team on their page. And if you have the knowledge and time, or know someone who does, the book cart drill team could have a web page of its very own. The next time you are surfing, type in "book cart drill team" and see what you get.

Then, what about national television? Lynne Zeiher's dream is for Pierce County Library's book cart drill team to be invited to appear on David Letterman's show. And why not? (The fact that the show is filmed in New York City and they are 3,000 miles away in Washington State shouldn't be a deterrent, should it?) What a way to break the stodgy stereotypical image of librarians.

Although Pierce County Library's Top 10 list of reasons why the drill team should appear on *The Late Show* has never received a positive response from the show's producers, it never hurts to ask. Try sending a story, complete with video, to the show's producers. Pick shows that you think may be receptive and focus on sending them a good story.

The Ocean County Library in New Jersey did get a bite from the Rosie O'Donnell show. The show's producers even asked for a video of the group. The Ocean County folks had a great time having a professional video made and are, at press time, still waiting for the thumbs-up from Rosie. Who knows what may happen next? Keep watching Letterman and Rosie for the national premiere of someone's book cart drill team.

· 13 ·

They're Everywhere!
Book Cart Drill Teams
Across North America

Fairfax City Regional Library, Fairfax, Virginia

They say great minds think alike, so it's no wonder that library book cart drill teams have sprung up all over the country. Actually, they popped up years before we started our teams in Gig Harbor and Yakima.

The very first library book cart drill team appears to have been started in 1983 by Joy Sibley, while at the Fairfax City Regional Library. According to Suzanne Levy, their precision book cart drill team has performed in many Fourth of July parades, as well as in a few "Gross National Parades," which are held, not too surprisingly, in Georgetown in the District of Columbia. The historically inclined may want to check out the photo in the September 1991 issue of the PLA Bulletin showing the West Shore Public Library.

The first Fairfax team was formed in response to a need to publicize the move from a branch in need of renovation to its temporary quarters. Now the summer reading game often shares top billing, as volunteers dressed as storybook characters or perhaps jugglers (depending on the theme) march along the parade route with the carts.

St. Joseph County Public Library, South Bend, Indiana

A decade or so later, another book cart drill team materialized in South Bend, Indiana. The then head of adult services at St. Joseph County Public Library, Larry Ostrowski, donned his drill sergeant uniform (complete with plumed hat) and led their 20 members in the Ethnic Festival parade. Marching abreast down the street, their carts spelled out a collection of four different phrases, such as "Read More!" Occasionally they would stop, twirl their carts in unison and form another phrase.

Santa Cruz City-County Library System, Santa Cruz, California

If a trend is hip, it's bound to show up somewhere in California. Naturally, book cart drill teams made it here too. According to librarian Anne Turner, Santa Cruz City-County Library System launched their team in the Santa Cruz Holiday Parade in December 1997. This group is lucky enough to have red book carts, which are festive anytime and particularly appropriate in their Christmas parade. The team repeats the holiday theme by wearing red and white Santa hats. In other parades they trade their Santa chapeaux for baseball caps. Their leader, who was a high school drum major, wears his old drum major gold braided jacket with jeans or Bermuda shorts in the summer. Sounds *très chic*. He even has a drum major's staff.

Alaska Library Association

Way up the West Coast in Alaska a group of six brave souls, including Patience Frederickson, put together an indoor performance team. Following the instructions of their square dance–like caller, they sashayed around and around for a gathering at the Alaska Library Association. Since they were indoors, they could easily use music (Dolly Parton singing "Nine to Five") and props. Each team member was equipped with a large picture book that they skillfully tossed, passed and even read in response to the caller's instructions.

Lincoln Library, Springfield, Illinois

Back in the Midwest, Nancy Huntley at the Lincoln Library of Springfield, Illinois, has taken book cart drill teaming to a new level. Their Cart Wheelers (a great name) put together a small booklet highlighting their adventures on the road. Individual creativity appears to be highly encouraged in this team, as each member decorates his/her cart in their own fashion, and their routines include time for personal improvisations. The booklet features a collection of photographs showing off their creative cart decorations, including

The Lincoln Library Cart Wheelers team photograph (photograph by Julie Wullner).

one with Big Bird reading his favorite book. Other photos illustrate their team members, who are obviously having a lot of fun, "surfing" on the carts and doing other fun stuff. Annette Hunsaker is proudly pictured marching along wearing her majorette skirt and waving her official looking baton. In true library style, each page of their tome is highlighted with inspiring literary quotes.

Annette Hunsaker makes a striking team leader and charming Christmas elf (photograph by Julie Wullner).

Among their original moves is the Skate, where they ride a cart like a scooter.

Bettendorf Public Library, Bettendorf, Iowa

Library book cart drill teams have even made it to the Internet. The drill team of the Bettendorf Public Library was featured on their website, but due to the changing nature of the Internet, they have since been replaced with a picture of the library's award-winning float. At one time they had several pictures showing off their attractive all-blue outfits and great cart decorations. Their first parade appearance was in their local Halloween parade. According to Nancy Medma, they were also accompanied by the library's costumed bear, named "Booker Bear." A picture of him is still featured on the website. Perhaps the drill team will be back on the Net sometime soon.

Ocean County Library, Ocean, New Jersey

In addition to perhaps being on the *Rosie O'Donnell Show*, the Ocean County Library has been immortalized in the following poetic tribute.

Group picture of the Ocean County Library Cart Wheelers (photograph by Jennifer Carling).

Ode to a Drill Cart Team
By Kathy Falco, Ocean County Library

Twist and turn with our magical carts—
All of us playing our own special part.
The routine is forming and off we go
To do our best for the show!!

Right turn, left turn, we feel the vibration,
The roar of the crowd our only libation.
People are smiling and cheering us on;
You can still hear them calling long after we're gone.

Marching side by side or in single file,
We'll be doing the Cobra in a little while.
"Toot Toot" goes the whistle and that's our cue—
We have to switch to a routine that's new!!

Double Snake wide—then form two lines,
Listen for the whistle—it gives us our signs
Of what to do next and which direction to take,
Stepping together for the drill team's sake!!

The end is coming and the arms are numb–
But we'll be missing the wheels' little hum.
Now the end is here and we must turn in our carts—
But all of our performances will remain in our hearts!!

And Still More

In our travels over the Internet, especially with the help of the Library Listserve, we have been able to identify and contact numerous other book cart drill teams sprinkled across the country. Fabulous teams have been parading around towns in the following areas:

Abilene Public Library, Abilene, Texas (headed by Dennis Miller)
Bozeman Public Library, Bozeman, Montana (Cindy Christin)
Butler County Federated Library System, Butler, Pennsylvania
     (Sheila Brown)

Calument City Public Library, Calument City, Illinois (Vickie L. Novak)

Carroll County Public Library, Eldersburg, Maryland (Kathy MacMillen)

Eugene Public Library, Eugene, Oregon (Patricia Dunham)

Everett Public Library, Everett, Washington (Jody Davis)

Flathead County Library, Kalispell, Montana (Anne James and Michael Hutchinson)

Geneva Public Library District, Geneva, Illinois (Nancy H. Bell)

Grace A. Dow Memorial Library, Midland, Michigan (Mary Fellows)

Kitsap Regional Library, Bremerton, Washington (Robin Cameron)

Missoula Public Library, Missoula, Montana (Karen Rehard)

Peter White Public Library, Marquette, Michigan (Bryn Smith)

Richland Public Library, Richland, Washington (Jeanette Mercier)

The Flathead County Library Truckers making wonderful Montana memories (photograph by Thomas E. Laird).

Canada

Not to be outdone by their neighbors to the south, Canadian libraries have taken to the streets as well. Book cart drill teams have been formed, from the E. Gwillimbury Public Library in Holland Landing, Ontario (Karen McLean), to the Greater Victoria Public Library in Victoria, British Columbia (Neil McAllister).

It's Not Just for Libraries Anymore

Boxlight Company, a library vendor selling computer projection units and other computer peripherals, has also jumped on the rolling drill team band wagon, so to speak. They don't have library book carts, but they have wheeled their projector cases out onto the streets of Poulsbo, Washington, for the Viking Fest Parade. A briefcase drill team inspired them first, but since they have utilized rolling units, book cart drill team maneuvers could easily be adjusted to make their potential future parade performances very special.

There are countless other organizations and tools that could also be used for a fun drill team performance. Grocery store carts, hospital carts, or even lawn mowers can hit the streets in style. The possibilities are endless.

· 14 ·

Happily Ever After:
The Story of the
Seven Noisy Carts

Once upon a time in a library not too far away there lived seven noisy carts. The librarians called them Squeaky, Squawky, Chirpy, Rattley, Squealy, Screechy and Hideous.

It was sad that they were so noisy, because in library land, quiet was the thing to be. They hadn't always been noisy; but after years of devoted service hauling books to and fro, the weight of it all had caused their wheels and joints to squeak and rattle. Still, they did their job day in and day out, even though they frequently suffered the stares and shushes of the library patrons and pages.

Occasionally they were treated to a squirt of WD40 on their achy wheels, but the treatments only temporarily hushed their rumble. They felt doomed to rattle as they rolled until their final days when they would be surplused and hauled to the local landfill or salvage yard. Alas.

One day a strange thing happened. The noisy carts were gathered together and rolled outside. Fear overcame them as they were pushed through the side door of the library and out into the parking lot.

"This is it," they thought. "The landfill for sure." Soon they were being pushed and spun in all directions. At first they were scared. This was nothing like the straight and plodding course they were used to—slowly inching from aisle to aisle loaded with heavy books. Now they were light and quick. The movements made them all a bit giddy. It wasn't long before the carts were gathered again and hustled back into the library. They weren't going to the landfill after all!

This event occurred several more times. Then an even stranger thing happened. Ribbons and signs and balloons were attached to the carts. The carts had never been adorned in such finery. Overwhelmed by their new fancy costumes, it took them a while to realize that they had left the library's parking lot and were rolling down a city street.

The surface of the street was rougher than the smooth library carpet, and it made the seven noisy carts rattle even louder than normal. But, much to their surprise, nobody seemed to mind. In fact, the people were uncharacteristically boisterous themselves. They were lining the street and actually cheering for the noisy book carts. That's when the noisy carts realized that they were in a parade, and, in fact, were the stars of the library's new book cart drill team.

All was not easy, though, in this strange new world. There were perilous obstacles along the way. They had to swerve and dodge to avoid the odorous piles left by the equestrian unit just ahead of them. Large potholes and deeply rutted railroad tracks threatened to trap them. With the help of the librarians, they were lifted over with ease.

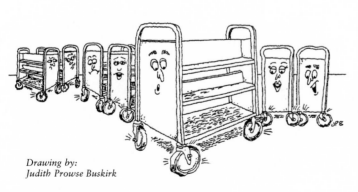

Drawing by:
Judith Prowse Buskirk

When the parade was over, they were happy to return to the quiet library knowing they had fulfilled their destiny and brought fame and friends to the library they loved.

Appendix A

Sample Parade Rules and Applications

The following are examples of parade rules and entry application forms. The first example is from a very small town. The rules are few and there is no entry fee. This was the first parade that the Yakima Valley Regional Library drill team appeared in. Our unique entry was very well received.

The second example is from a much larger town. The rules are really quite elaborate, but the process of entry, assembling, and the parade itself flows very smoothly—thanks in large part to the preparation time.

The Zillah Parade Committee is pleased to invite you to participate in the Zillah Parade on our Community Day, which is held every year on the second Saturday in May. We would appreciate it if you would return the enclosed entry form no later than **MAY 5 th , 1999** This will ensure you a proper place in the parade. **LATE ENTRIES WILL NOT BE ACCEPTED AFTER MAY 7th.**

ASSEMBLY AREAS:

Please check in at the registration booth located on First Avenue near the softball field and on the same side of the road. Here you will get directions to your assigned area for assembling of your unit. Area is opened by 7:00 a.m.

JUDGING:

Judging of all entries will commence at 8:30 a.m. in the assembly area and end at 10:30 a.m. As the bands and drill teams are judged enroute on appearance and marching, the judging will take place in the vicinity of the announcing platform which is located on 2nd Avenue.

AWARDS:

Except for the bands and drill teams, all awards will be presented in the assembly areas prior to the beginning of the parade.

HANDOUTS:

Due to the danger to children, throwing of candy, posters or paper of any kind, will be **PROHIBITED**. Only persons walking may pass out any material.

PLEASE SEND ENTRY FORM AND REQUESTS FOR ADDITIONAL INFORMATION TO:

AMERICAN LEGION
P.O.B 603
ZILLAH, WA 98953
PHONE: 509-829-5606 OR 509-829-5199

146

Sample Parade Rules and Applications

ZILLAH COMMUNITY DAY

Always the second Saturday in May

PARADE ENTRY BLANK

The registration booth will be at the entrance to the baseball fields located on First Avenue. Judging is from 8:30 a.m. to 10:00 a.m. Registration is from 7:00 a.m. to 10:30 a.m.

DEADLINE for parade entries is May 7th. Parade will be on May 8th.

TYPE OF ENTRY: (check one) Car/pick-up_____ Band _____ Drill team _____
Horses_____ Float _____ Misc. _____

Person in charge of entry _____

Description and theme of entry in detail (if entry is a float, give names of persons riding on float. If entry is a Drill group, please give number of persons, captain, and Major (ettes), etc.)

_____

_____

_____

_____

INDEMNITY AND HOLD HARMLESS

_____ agrees to indemnify, hold harmless and defend any action against the Zillah Community Day Festival from and against all liabilities whatsoever arising out it it's participation in the Zillah Community Day Parade.

Organization, Individual or Firm _____

Date _____ Signature of Person in Charge _____
                                                              Title _____

_____   _____
(address of entrant)   (phone number)

_____
                                          PLEASE SEND YOUR ENTRY IN BY MAY 7TH.

ZILLAH AMERICAN LEGION
P.O.B. 603 ZILLAH, WA. 98953
PHONE 509-829-5199 OR 509-829-5606

147

1999 SELAH COMMUNITY DAYS PARADE ENTRY APPLICATION

<u>ENTRY DEADLINE:</u> - MAY 8 1999

<u>PARADE DATE:</u> - MAY 22 1999

<u>PARADE TIMES:</u> - (SIGN IN 6:30am.)   (STAGING START 7:00am)   (JUDGING START 8:00am.)
(PARADE START 10:00am.)
If you wish to be judged you must be in place in the staging area by 8:00am (see map)

NAME OF ENTRY:_____

SPONSOR:_____

CONTACT PERSON:_____

ADDRESS:_____

CITY:_____STATE:_____ZIP:_____

PHONE: DAY:_____ NIGHT: _____E-MAIL:_____

NEXT YRS CONTACT:_____NEXT YRS PHONE:_____

NEXT YEARS ADDRESS:_____CITY_____ZIP_____

After reading "Parade Divisions Defined" included in the packet. Enter the name of the division in which you wish to be entered in the space below. (The parade coordinator reserves the right to change the division selected if it is felt the entry is better suited in another division)

DIVISION TO BE ENTERED IN:_____

After reading the rules please attache the appropriate Entry Fee, Certificate of Insurance and Narrative with this application...

[ ] **Entry Fee attached (see rule 15)**

[ ] **Certificate of Insurance attached (see rule 16 & the back of the Cruise Night Infro. sheet)**

[ ] **Narrative attached (See the back of this application)**

[ ] **Pooper Scooper information attached (see rule 14, and the back of this application)**

It is important to include the approximate number of Cars in Club, Band Members, Marchers, Horses, Etc. In your Group!   _____

I certify that I have read all the rules for the Selah Community Days Parade and agree to abide by them. My signature indicates my understanding of these rules and indicates a desire to participate in this event. All members of my organization taking part in this event have been notified of those rules. In consideration of the acceptance of our entry, the sponsor and/or parade participant(s) named herein, here-by indemnify and hold harmless the Selah Community Days Association, City of Selah, and Washington State Highway Department and their officers and employees, from any claim or demand for personal injury, death or property damages which arise through or in connection with the sponsor's and/or parade participant's participation in the Selah Community Days Parade.

SIGNATURE:_____   DATE:_____

* * * COMPLETE BOTH FRONT AND BACK OF APPLICATION * * *

Sample Parade Rules and Applications

ANNOUNCERS' NARRATIVE

<u>PLEASE TYPE OR PRINT LEGIBLY</u>
USE SEPARATE PAPER If NEEDED
These are just sugestions of things to include in your marrative.
Feel free to say anything you would like about your entry!

Description of Unit:

Individuals to be Recognized:

Other Comments to be Mentioned, Awards etc:

Parade announcers have only about one minute to comment on each unit. To insure the narrative includes everything you would like said about your unit or organization, you should limit your comments to a total of about 100 words or less. Although we will make every effort to announce everything you would like said about your entry and/or organization, we reserve the right to edit your comments as to length.

****

SUPER POOPER SCOOPER ENTRY APPLICATION

<u>Required for all Equestrian and Animal units (see rule 14)</u>

Name:

Unit(s) Cleaning Up After:

Theme or Description (optional):

Other Comments to be Mentioned (optional):

<u>Mail completed Parade Entry Application and applicable paper work to.</u>

SELAH COMMUNITY DAYS
PARADE COMMITTEE
P.O.BOX 783
SELAH, WA 98942

For additional information contact: Alan Pelzel,

Days - 697-7735, Nights - 697-8274, Cell - 949-6563, e-mail - ALPEL@prodigy.net
Web Page - http://pages.prodigy.net/alpel/selahcommunitydays.index.htm

Additional packets can be obtained at City Hall and the Civic Center

----

PLEASE TAKE I-82 TO EXIT #26 THE YAKIMA TRAINING CENTER EXIT, TURN LEFT AT THE STOP SIGN (RIGHT FROM ELLENSBURG). TAKE THE NEXT LEFT ON TO HARRISON RD AND FOLLOW IT TO THE STOP SIGN. TURN LEFT AND GO TO THE STOP LIGHT. THE STAGING AREA IS IN THE SAVE-ON-FOODS PARKING LOT.

ACORD. CERTIFICATE OF LIABILITY INSURANCE

DATE (MM/DD/YY)
03/30/98

PRODUCER	THIS CERTIFICATE IS ISSUED AS A MATTER OF INFORMATION ONLY AND CONFERS NO RIGHTS UPON THE CERTIFICATE HOLDER. THIS CERTIFICATE DOES NOT AMEND, EXTEND OR ALTER THE COVERAGE AFFORDED BY THE POLICIES BELOW.
INSURANCE COMPANY NAME HERE	**COMPANIES AFFORDING COVERAGE**
	COMPANY A
INSURED	COMPANY B
YOUR NAME HERE	COMPANY C
	COMPANY D

COVERAGES

THIS IS TO CERTIFY THAT THE POLICIES OF INSURANCE LISTED BELOW HAVE BEEN ISSUED TO THE INSURED NAMED ABOVE FOR THE POLICY PERIOD INDICATED, NOTWITHSTANDING ANY REQUIREMENT, TERM OR CONDITION OF ANY CONTRACT OR OTHER DOCUMENT WITH RESPECT TO WHICH THIS CERTIFICATE MAY BE ISSUED OR MAY PERTAIN, THE INSURANCE AFFORDED BY THE POLICIES DESCRIBED HEREIN IS SUBJECT TO ALL THE TERMS, EXCLUSIONS AND CONDITIONS OF SUCH POLICIES. LIMITS SHOWN MAY HAVE BEEN REDUCED BY PAID CLAIMS.

CO LTR	TYPE OF INSURANCE	POLICY NUMBER	POLICY EFFECTIVE DATE (MM/DD/YY)	POLICY EXPIRATION DATE (MM/DD/YY)	LIMITS	
	GENERAL LIABILITY	LIABILITY POLICY # HERE			GENERAL AGGREGATE	$
	COMMERCIAL GENERAL LIABILITY				PRODUCTS - COMP/OP AGG	$
	CLAIMS MADE / OCCUR				PERSONAL & ADV INJURY	$
	OWNER'S & CONTRACTOR'S PROT				EACH OCCURRENCE	$
					FIRE DAMAGE (Any one fire)	$
					MED EXP (Any one person)	$
A	AUTOMOBILE LIABILITY	POLICY NUMBER HERE	11/04/97	11/04/98	COMBINED SINGLE LIMIT	500,000
	ANY AUTO					
	ALL OWNED AUTOS				BODILY INJURY (Per person)	$
X	SCHEDULED AUTOS					
	HIRED AUTOS				BODILY INJURY (Per accident)	$
	NON-OWNED AUTOS				PROPERTY DAMAGE	$
	GARAGE LIABILITY				AUTO ONLY - EA ACCIDENT	$
	ANY AUTO				OTHER THAN AUTO ONLY:	
					EACH ACCIDENT	$
					AGGREGATE	$
	EXCESS LIABILITY				EACH OCCURRENCE	$
	UMBRELLA FORM				AGGREGATE	$
	OTHER THAN UMBRELLA FORM					
	WORKERS COMPENSATION AND EMPLOYERS' LIABILITY				WC STATU- TORY LIMITS / OTH- ER	
	THE PROPRIETOR/ PARTNERS/EXECUTIVE INCL OFFICERS ARE EXCL				EL EACH ACCIDENT	$
					EL DISEASE-POLICY LIMIT	$
	OTHER				EL DISEASE EA EMPLOYEE	$

Example

DESCRIPTION OF OPERATIONS/LOCATIONS/VEHICLES/SPECIAL ITEMS

EVENT - SELAH COMMUNITY DAYS PARADE
LIST OF VEHICLE'S ETC THAT WILL BE IN PARADE

CERTIFICATE HOLDER	CANCELLATION
THE CITY OF SELAH AND STATE HIGHWAY DEPARTMENT AND SELAH COMMUNITY DAYS ASSOC PO BOX 783, SELAH WA 98942	SHOULD ANY OF THE ABOVE DESCRIBED POLICIES BE CANCELLED BEFORE THE EXPIRATION DATE THEREOF, THE ISSUING COMPANY WILL ENDEAVOR TO MAIL 10 DAYS WRITTEN NOTICE TO THE CERTIFICATE HOLDER NAMED TO THE LEFT, BUT FAILURE TO MAIL SUCH NOTICE SHALL IMPOSE NO OBLIGATION OR LIABILITY OF ANY KIND UPON THE COMPANY, ITS AGENTS OR REPRESENTATIVES. AUTHORIZED REPRESENTATIVE

Sample Parade Rules and Applications

SELAH COMMUNITY DAYS PARADE
RULES AND REGULATIONS

1. Entrants must observe all applicable rules and regulations and follow all instructions from police or parade officials. The Selah Community Days Association and the Parade Committee reserve the right to remove any entrant from the parade either prior to assembly, at assembly or at any time during the parade.

2. Floats, or any other units, advocating, opposing or depicting any social or religious issues are subject to approval of the Selah Community Days Parade Committee.

3. **The Selah Community Days Association and its Parade Committee reserve the right to withdraw any unit of which the costume or performance does not meet these rules and regulations, or does not conform to the standards of reasonable community taste and decency.**

4. The Parade Committee's decision regarding all entrants, their eligibility, placement and judging is final.

5. Entries are by invitation only and must be approved by the Parade Committee.

6. Parade applications received after the published entry deadline my not be eligible for judging or awards.

7. No water is permitted in the parade, in conjunction with floats or otherwise, except with permission of the Selah Community Days Association Parade Committee.

8. Alcoholic beverages are forbidden on any float, vehicle or on the person of any parade participant. No profanity is allowed along the parade route or within the assembly areas.

9. **No materials (candy etc.) will be thrown along the parade route.** Walkers my hand out candy to parade spectators with permission. Distribution of gifts, merchandise, literature or any other material is prohibited, except with permission of the Selah Community Days Parade Committee.

10. Parade participants may not mingle with or accost parade spectators.

11. Only forward movement maneuvers are permitted along the parade route. A spacing of 40 feet between each unit will be enforced. All units are required to open or close the gap between units when asked to do so by parade officials.

12. Entries that do not appear on parade day without prior notification, or do not fully comply with the rules and regulations, jeopardize future invitations to the Selah Community Days.

13. The Selah Community Days Association does not accept the responsibility for traveling expenses, food, lodging or any other expenses of the parade entrant.

14. All equestrian units or other units with live animals, **must provide their own clean up crew.** also see rule 16 An award will be presented in this division.

15. **Political candidates, political organizations, commercial businesses,** and any for profit organization will be charged a **$50.00 entry fee.** Contributions made to Selah Community Days may be applied toward this entry fee at the discretion of the Selah Community Days Board upon the request of the applicant.

16. All vehicles with an engine or motor and all units having live animals, including equestrian units, must provide evidence of insurance for bodily injury and property damage with a combined single limit of $300,000 or split limits of $250,000 each person and $500,000 each occurrence bodily injury liability and $100,000 property damage liability. **A certificate of insurance must be provided with, Selah Community Days Association, City of Selah and the Washington State Highway Dept. named as additional insured.** This certificate of insurance must be received with your entry application. See the back of the Cruise Night information sheet of an example of the Certificate of Insurance.

151

IMPORTANT REMINDERS

PARADE DATE: MAY 22
ENTRY DEAD LINE: MAY 8
SIGN IN STARTS: 6:30am
JUDGING STARTS: 8:00am
PARADE STARTS: 10:00am

* *

ANY VEHICLE THAT HAS AN ENGINE OR MOTOR IS **REQUIRED** TO HAVE INSURANCE BEFORE BEING ALLOWED TO ENTER.

THE SELAH COMMUNITY DAYS ASSOCIATION, CITY OF SELAH AND THE WASHINGTON STATE HIGHWAY DEPARTMENT **MUST BE** NAMED AS ADDITIONAL INSURED ON YOUR CERTIFICATE OF INSURANCE. (See the back of Cruise Night sheet for example)

ANY UNIT CONTAINING ANY LIVE ANIMALS, INCLUDING ALL EQUESTRIAN UNITS,ARE **REQUIRED** TO HAVE INSURANCE AND PROVIDE A CERTIFICATE OF INSURANCE.

Although the Insurance requirement sounds complicated or difficult and costly. It is generally a quite easy requirement to meet. Simply go to your insurance agent and show him/her (rule 16). We have talked with a number of insurance agents and all have told us that there would be no charge for this certificate of insurance unless you do not already carry this base limit (rule 16) on your home, farm or car insurance. There may be a small charge if you need to increase your insurance coverage for the one day. If your agent has any questions have them call Alan Pelzel at 697-7735 or 949-6863. There is an example of the Certificate of Insurance form on the back of the Cruise Night information sheet.

* *

ANY UNIT CONTAINING ANY LIVE ANIMALS, INCLUDING ALL EQUESTRIAN UNITS, MUST PROVIDE THEIR OWN CLEAN UP CREW BEFORE BEING ALLOWED TO ENTER.

* *

ALL COMMERCIAL AND POLITICAL ENTRIES MUST PAY A $50.00 ENTRY FEE !

* *

CANDY CAN NOT BE THROWN ALONG THE PARADE ROUTE!

The throwing of candy along the parade route has been prohibited in Selah for many years. This rule is to protect the safety of both spectators and participants. It will be strictly enforced! Walkers my hand out candy to parade spectators with permission.

* *

If you would like something said about your entry,
complete the Announcers Narrative on the back of the Application form!

* *

Check out Selah Community Days web site for more information.
and this complete parade packet.

http://pages.prodigy.net/alpel/selahcommunitydays.index.htm

152

Appendix B

How to Make Book Clappers

Those who cringe at the sight of a torn book might not want to read this section. It contains instructions on how to create "book clappers" that can be swirled and twirled by extra members of the book cart drill team. Making them is easy, but does involve what might be viewed as book abuse by some.

Start with a small to medium sized hardback book that is ready for retirement. Reader's Digest Condensed books are about the right size. Open the book in the middle. Now here comes the queasy part. Cut approximately ½" thickness of pages from the center of the book as close to the spine as possible without cutting the spine webbing. Use two pieces of ¼" thick plywood, trimmed slightly smaller than the length and width of the pages. Attach these pieces of plywood to the inside of the book on each side where you cut out the center pages. Insert flat head drywall screws through the hard cover into the plywood.

This secures the plywood and the loose pages. This type of screw is self-counter sinking, so the head doesn't stick out. It may be difficult to obtain wood screws exactly long enough to accomplish the step. If the screws are too long, grind off the point of the screw that protrudes through the plywood.

Cut one or two 1" thick dowels into 4" lengths. These dowels

Figure 1

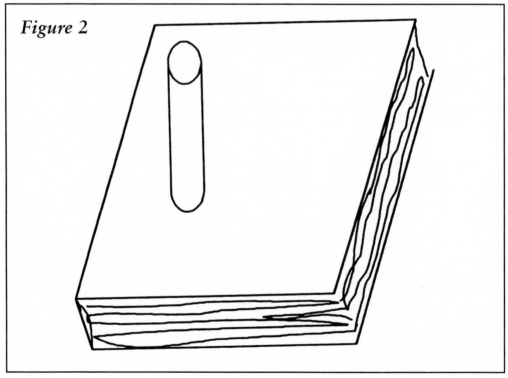

Figure 2

will be attached to the outside of the book using a wood screw from the inside. Attaching the dowel offset from the center of the cover makes the book easier to spin one-handed. Countersink a hole large enough to allow the head to be recessed but also to ensure that there is sufficient wood remaining in the ¼" plywood to hold the screw head. Drill a preliminary hole through the center of one end of the dowel to prevent it from splitting when the screw is installed. Do not tighten the screw very tight. It should be loose enough to allow the book to spin when holding onto the handle.

Two dowels, one on each side of the book, make holding and clapping it easier, but are a bit less attractive and book looking. The second dowel can also present a hazard to the body while spinning. If using only one dowel, it's helpful to have a smaller book that enables the holder to grasp the cover by the edges with the fingers and thumb.

The plywood insert produces a loud "clap" sound. Old-fashioned furniture tacks can also be hammered into the plywood, opposite one another, to create a louder clicking sound when the books are clapped together.

Index

Numbers in *italics* refer to photographs.

157

Index

Index

Index